The Landlord's Guide to
Student Letting

If you want to know how. . .

The New Landlord's Guide to Letting
How to buy and let residential property for profit

The Beginner's Guide to Property Investment
The ultimate handbook for first-time buyers and would-be property investors

How to Buy a Flat
All you need to know on apartment living and letting

How to Buy and Let a Holiday Cottage

How to be a Property Millionaire

howtobooks

Send for a free copy of the latest catalogue to:

How To Books
Spring Hill House, Spring Hill Road,
Begbroke, Oxford OX5 1RX. United Kingdom.
info@howtobooks.co.uk
www.howtobooks.co.uk

The Landlord's Guide to
Student Letting

How to find an investment property
and let it out to students

Catherine Bancroft-Rimmer

howto books

Published by How To Books Ltd,
Spring Hill House, Spring Hill Road,
Begbroke, Oxford OX5 1RX. United Kingdom.
Tel: (01865) 375794. Fax: (01865) 379162.
info@howtobooks.co.uk
www.howtobooks.co.uk

British Library Cataloguing in Publication Data
A catalogue record for this book is available from the British Library

ISBN 978 1 84528 189 2

Cover illustration and cartoons by David Mostyn
Cover design by Baseline Arts Ltd, Oxford
Produced for How To Books by Deer Park Productions, Tavistock, Devon
Typeset by PDQ Typesetting, Newcastle-under-Lyme, Staffs.
Printed and bound by Bell & Bain Ltd, Glasgow

Contents

Preface

For any but the most confident investor, starting off in property letting can be a bewildering minefield of legislation and financial risk. If you are considering the student letting market you may also be worried about the perceived image of students as exemplified by the popular 1980s TV programme, *The Young Ones*. The fact that many student tenants are equally wary of the image of landlords based on the character of Rigsby from another popular sitcom, *Rising Damp*, means that this area can have serious worries for both parties of a prospective tenancy agreement!

However, despite the perceived image, letting to students can be a rewarding and financially beneficial way of investing in property. The government has stated its aim of increasing the student population to 50% of 18–30 year olds by 2010 and many universities have started a building programme to meet this increased demand. However, the financial burden of doing so, as well as the desire of many returning students to be independent of the more restrictive regime in halls of residence, has meant that the private rented sector continues to be a source of reliance for most students looking for somewhere to live.

This book will take you through the pros and cons of letting to students in the UK[1] and explains the nuts and bolts of letting,

---

1   Any legislation referred to throughout the book is usually only applicable to England and Wales. Landlords investing in Scotland or Northern Ireland will need to check how the law relates to their area separately.

with a particular emphasis on letting to groups of young people studying in higher or further education. Attention will also be paid to how university accommodation departments can help in both marketing and managing your property. With any sector of tenants there will inevitably be problems that crop up – this book will deal with the most common ones relating to students and how best to deal with them.

As a private landlord myself, as well as someone who has been a student accommodation manager at two popular universities, I am aware that there is a need for a clear and comprehensive handbook for those landlords who are entering the student letting market for the first time. Even for those of you who may have been letting to students for many years, the market and the legislation are constantly changing and it is ever more important that you ensure you are operating within the law and keep up to date with how you can best market your investment and remain competitive in the face of the increasing amount of purpose built student accommodation.

Catherine Bancroft-Rimmer LLM
www.cbr-studentinvestments.co.uk

Acknowledgements

Thanks are due to all those who have given me help and advice over the years I have been involved in student housing, in particular those landlords registered with the University of Sussex whose concerns and questions have informed much of the content of this book. Thanks are also due to my manager, Lorinda Holness, and colleagues in the Housing Office at Sussex, who have put up with a certain amount of absent-mindedness on my part while I was finishing this text. I am particularly thankful for the help and guidance of Andrew Faber, who was a fine friend and landlord, and who encouraged me to become personally involved in letting properties to students.

Many thanks go to my two sons, Tom and Alex, who graciously allowed me to use the computer when they were desperate to play their latest game. Thanks also to my parents for their love and encouragement. Last, but not least, enormous gratitude to my partner, Tim Huitson, for his patient advice, support and extensive proof-reading. Any mistakes in grammar are now entirely his!

Why Let to Students?

IN THIS CHAPTER

Government influences and demographic changes

Buying for your student offspring

Students are young, messy and financially compromised – why would any landlord in their right mind want to let to students? It's certainly true that students present a more demanding set of challenges than a professional couple. For one thing, it is either their first time living away from home (and you can bet that most of them have no idea how to run a household) or, secondly, they may have spent a year cocooned in the safety of a university residence with their cleaning done weekly, loo rolls and light bulbs provided and a team of staff trained specifically to deal with the issues arising when a large group of young people live together.

As a professional with a primary interest in making sure that your large financial investment makes you a reasonable return, you are probably not in a position, nor have the desire, to provide the level of service to your tenants that an educational institution would.

However, there are a number of reasons why letting to students isn't such a bad idea:

- You can fit more in per house (a house with two reception rooms could have one of those converted to a study bedroom).

- They will live in areas that other tenants turn their noses up at (as long as they can catch a bus to their study site easily).

- They don't expect power showers, frosted glass sinks or infinity pools – although they'd probably like them!

- They will put up with swirly carpets and flock wallpaper if the property is in the right area.

- They are not averse to paying rent three months in advance.

- Often it is the more financially viable parents who are paying the rent for them.

- They are, on the whole (there are exceptions), intelligent and therefore quick to grasp whatever it is you are trying to tell them.

- No problem with sitting tenants – students move out when the tenancy ends (or their course does).

Notwithstanding the advantages, some landlords really can't cope with letting to students – mainly because their personality isn't flexible enough to put up with the disadvantages that letting to students present. If any of the following would cause you to lie awake at night worrying, or cause you to grind your teeth with frustration, then letting to students probably isn't for you.

- One of your student's standing order payments has failed and he wants to pay this month's rent in cash, but he hasn't got the right change.

- There are some items missing at the end of the tenancy from the detailed inventory you provided – which includes items such as teaspoons, designer vases and dusters.

- When you leave a message with one member of the household to say that you will be coming round to inspect next week, the others are not aware of it and look blankly at you when you turn up.

- You think the best time to carry out inspections is at 9.30am and you can't understand why most of the bedrooms are smelly, dark and have comatose students still in bed – sometimes with someone else.

- Despite requesting that you are only contacted out of office hours in an emergency, you still receive telephone calls late in the evening informing you that the dustbin has gone missing.

Also, if your view of students extends to any of the following, it's probably best you consider letting to other sectors.

- You can't see the point of providing a clean house at the beginning of a let, because you think students are all dirty anyway and won't mind.

- You will only let to a group of students if you can carry out a monthly inspection and then lecture on the state of cleanliness of the property.

- You have no compunction about lecturing students on the morality of whether they can have boyfriends/girlfriends to stay.

- You will not let to international students on principle.

- You have a problem with letting to ethnic minorities, gays, bisexuals or people practising certain religions.

- You don't believe in 'fair wear and tear'.

- All students are lazy layabouts who should be out in the real world earning a living.

If you are still interested in reading the rest of this book after this section, then you are probably going to cope fine with letting to students and may even get some satisfaction out of providing a decent home to a young, intelligent, idealistic group of people educating themselves so they can earn enough to provide your pension.

GOVERNMENT INFLUENCES AND DEMOGRAPHIC CHANGES

As a property purchase is normally a long-term investment, it is prudent to be aware of how the market you are in may change over the longer term. I mentioned earlier that the government's intention is to have 50% participation in higher education by 2010. With this aim it is more or less certain that demand for private sector accommodation for students will continue to be buoyant for the next five years at least, for the reasons I mentioned in the introduction. However, this does raise two more questions:

1. Is this figure achievable?
2. What happens after 2010?

Latest thinking seems to be indicating that 50% participation in HE by 2010 is not achievable. Basically, the government initiatives in school education and widening participation in HE have not produced the results hoped for. However, demography alone will ensure that the number of students at university will continue to increase between now and 2010. In addition, the enlargement of the EU will help to ensure that UK student populations will continue to increase – so long as universities are able to cope with those increases.

The only possible fly in the ointment is the impact of tuition fees but, at the time of writing (2006/2007), student applications to HE are still rising.

Longer term, demography indicates that the 18–21 age group in the UK population will begin to fall dramatically. (This effect has already been experienced in primary schools and can now be seen in Years 7–8 in secondary schools.) However, because this drop in the population is concentrated mainly in the social groups which do not traditionally attend university, its effect will not be so great in the HE sector as might be supposed. Nevertheless, it is anticipated that the student population in 2015 will only be marginally higher than it is in 2005/2006 and 2% less by 2020. If, however, the government manage to solve the problem of the number of young males not equalling young females in attending university, then the impact would actually be to increase the overall student population up to 2020 at least.

In the meantime universities are increasing the amount of accommodation they provide (either direct or through private sector companies such as Unite), which may have an impact on private sector demand. However, if you ensure that you invest in property which is in a popular student location and marketed well then you should be able to minimise voids. If, after a few years, you decide to get out of student letting, there will probably still be a large market of young professionals unable or unwilling to buy property of their own and looking to rent from experienced landlords who know what to provide.

BUYING FOR YOUR STUDENT OFFSPRING

You may be in the position of having a child about to start

university and are, therefore, considering whether you could save on rental costs by buying a property near to the university and letting to your son/daughter and some of his/her friends. Rental costs are one of the biggest expenses of going to university. Given that parents are usually the ones footing the bill, buying a property to let out to students in order to cover the rent of your offspring as well usually makes sense. It's a growing area. In 2006 approximately 82,000 homes were purchased by parents for their student offspring – a 26% increase since 2000.

If you do go down this route, it is worth putting some thought into whose name the house will go into. There are tax advantages to buying a house in your child's name. If the house is your child's primary residence then they won't have to pay capital gains tax on the property and, as long as your son or daughter does not breach their tax threshold, rental income can be offset against their personal tax allowance and they may also be able to claim a 'rent a room allowance'. See the tax section in Chapter 2 for more information on this. If you do not want to give complete control of the house over to your child you can set up a trust instead. This also has tax benefits but ensures that you still retain some control over the property.

Whether or not it makes sense to buy a house for your child does depend on the university town your child is going to be living in and how much money you need to borrow. Some areas, such as Nottingham and Liverpool, now have an oversupply of student accommodation and others, like Brighton, have property prices so high that, if you are 'highly geared' (borrowing a high percentage of the purchase price) the rents are unlikely to cover the mortgage payments. If you are in the very fortunate position of not needing to borrow much, then you only need to look at the projected growth in property values to see whether this will be a good investment for you.

In essence the northern university areas have experienced massive property price growth in the past few years, but are unlikely to do so again for a while. In addition, areas such as Manchester and Leeds have a lot of new build student accommodation. Southern towns have been unable to do this to the same extent because of the higher land prices.

Research the area

If you do decide to buy a property for your child and friends to live in, make sure you research the area carefully. It might be best to let your child live in university accommodation for the first year (if it is available), so that he or she gets to know the popular student areas before you decide to invest. There is also the possibility that he or she will decide that the university or course is not for them and drop out during the first year (peak drop out time is during November). If you have already bought a property for them to live in, it's going to make that decision harder.

SUMMARY

♦ There are advantages and disadvantages to letting to students. Are you flexible enough as an individual to cope with the disadvantages and profit from the advantages?

♦ The student population is predicted to continue to grow until 2010 at least. After that, it looks as though there may be up to a 2% decline until 2020. How do you plan to make sure that doesn't affect your returns?

◆ It can be financially very beneficial for you to purchase a property where your child is studying. If you are considering this, make sure you know what your returns are likely to be and what the likely capital growth is going to be over the period that you intend to keep the property.

◆ Wait until your child has been at university for a few months before deciding if and where to buy a property.

Buying a Property

IN THIS CHAPTER

Funding the purchase

Calculating the yield and capital growth

Selecting the town/city

Selecting the location and type of property

Deciding when to buy

Letting part of your own home

Tax matters

So you have made the decision to get a buy-to-let. Now you just need to work out how and where to do it. Many people have made a lot of money by taking advantage of the rapidly increasing value of property. However, now that prices have slowed down a bit, it is not as easy to make money quickly as it was a few years ago. You certainly need to take the long-term view and make sure you get the right property in the right location.

CASE STUDY_____

Maths teacher millionaires

In the early 1990s two maths teachers in Kent bought a property at auction with a £10,000 deposit. As property prices began to rise they were able to re-mortgage and use the increasing equity to buy more properties. They targeted Ashford in Kent, which had lower prices than surrounding areas, but was the site for the impending Eurostar terminal. They concentrated on buying new-build, small houses which could be let to professional couples and which did not have the problems associated with leasehold flats.

When interest only mortgages became available in 1996 they were able to expand even further and now have 700 properties at an estimated value of £240m.

FUNDING THE PURCHASE

It is important for me to state here that I am not a financial advisor and I strongly advocate that you get your own financial advice from a properly regulated independent financial advisor so that you can be sure of getting the best deal in the current market. However, I think it is worthwhile running through the basics of how you can get started in buy-to-let.

If you are fortunate enough to have a very large lump sum sitting in your bank account begging to be used, then you are going to find it relatively easy to invest in property. Although you may be able to afford to buy a property outright it is worth noting that it is tax efficient to have an interest-free loan for properties you let, as you can offset the interest payments against your income from the property. Therefore you may decide to invest part of your lump sum in a 20% deposit on a buy-to-let property and finance the rest with a buy-to-let mortgage. You may then choose to use the rest of the money to buy several properties in a similar way, or invest it in something other than property.

A buy-to-let mortgage is a relatively recent phenomenon. In the past people wanting to buy a property to let had to fund the full cost themselves, or get a repayment loan for part of the cost at a high rate from a specialist lender. The widespread introduction of interest-free buy-to-let loans from high street banks has revolutionised the market and has enabled many people who previously could not do so to invest in property.

Most buy-to-let mortgages at competitive rates ask for a 20 or 25% deposit, although some only ask for only 15%. Many people raise the deposit by increasing the mortgage on the home they are living in, thus releasing some of the equity that they have earned through increasing property prices.

CASE STUDY

Ms R

Ms R was keen to get involved in buy-to-let but did not have enough cash for the initial deposit. The mortgage on her own home was £60,000 but, due to the rapid increase in property prices over the previous few years, her property was now worth over £130,000. By making use of an independent mortgage broker she was able to find a lender who was prepared to lend up to 75% of the current value of her property, provided she was earning at least £20,000 per annum. By remortgaging for 75% of the value of her house, she was able to release approximately £40,000 in cash. She put £35,000 down as a deposit on a house around the corner that she bought for £150,000. The remaining £115,000 was funded by a buy-to-let mortgage. Three years later she was able to remortgage both her houses and raise enough deposit to buy a third. ■

Buy-to-let mortgages are almost always at a higher interest rate than a mortgage on a house you are going to live in. You will also need to decide whether you are going to take a fixed rate loan or a variable rate. A fixed rate may sound best if interest rates look likely to increase, however the banks will impose a higher interest rate on these. It might be worthwhile taking the risk of a variable rate mortgage, but putting extra money away each month so that you can fund any later interest rate increases yourself.

CALCULATING THE YIELD AND CAPITAL GROWTH

Now that you have your lump sum (or have worked out what it's going to be), and know how big a property you can afford, you need to work out whether it is worthwhile investing in a property or whether you are better off putting your money in some other investment (or just keeping it where it is!). There is a way of calculating the money you will be earning through property investment (yield) that enables you to compare it to any other investment. It works like this:

$$\frac{\text{Rent profit}}{\text{Current property value (including purchase costs)}} \times 100 = \text{Yield}$$

In order to get there you will have to put quite a bit of work into calculating what your profit is likely to be. First, you have to know what the annual rent is likely to be, building in a void period to be on the safe side. Second, you need to subtract your loan costs and any other estimated running costs, such as repairs, cleaning, safety checks, replacement of furniture, etc. Clearly the yield will vary from year to year, depending on how the different factors change.

	£
Here is an example:	
Estimated annual rent:	13,200
Less	
Interest on loan	5,000
Rates, insurance, bills, etc	400
Repairs, maintenance	550
Replacements (estimate at 10% of rent income)	1,320
Profit	5,930

Next, divide this amount by the current value of the property, plus purchase costs (i.e. solicitors' fees, stamp duty etc.) and anything extra you've had to pay to get it ready. Let's say that amount is £150,000:

$$\frac{£5,930}{£150,000} \times 100 = 3.95\%$$

Most landlords would be looking to get a return of between 6–9%, so whether you would proceed on this basis might depend on whether you could get better use from your money if you invested it elsewhere. Whether you go ahead may also depend on why you are buying the property. If you are buying because you have a son or daughter at university who will be living in it, then it may well be beneficial to you to go ahead anyway.

Capital growth

You also have to consider the impact of capital growth. This is the amount the property grows in value between the time you bought it to the time you sell, minus the costs associated with buying and selling.

For example, say you buy a property for £145,000, which costs you £150,00 by the time you start to let it. Three years later you sell it for £200,000, which gives you a net profit of £32,000 after allowing for selling costs and capital gains tax. That means that, over those three years, you have made a return of 21.33%, or 7.1% per year, which is probably more than you would have achieved if you had put the money in a savings account – particularly if you have made rental profits as well.

Hanging onto the property for longer can affect the rate of your capital growth if property prices slow down, however over time your yield will improve as rents increase in proportion to the value of the property. At some point in the future, capital growth will increase again and you may have a period of poor yields until rents catch up. As with any investment, it all depends on how much you buy for, what you sell for and how much you earn in between.

SELECTING THE TOWN/CITY

It may be that you have already made the decision on where to buy your property. This may be because you want to buy somewhere close enough for you to manage the let or because you want to buy in the university town that your son/daughter is studying in. If, however, you have a relatively open mind on where you buy it is worth doing a bit of research to ensure you get the best value for money.

There is a lot of talk about 'property hotspots'. There are even whole books devoted to the subject. There is not much point in going into detail here, however, as where a particular 'hotspot' is can change dramatically from one year to the next. Over the past five years the three best performing university towns in terms of capital growth have been Sunderland, Salford and Pontypridd[2] and most of the rest that performed well have been in the North, North/West, East Midlands and Wales. Those that have performed least well have been in London and the south east. However, at the time of writing, prices in London are picking up at the top end of the market and, if prices follow the same trend as in the past, this will start a new wave of price increases in the south east.

Top towns

For long-term growth in the student rental market you will need to take into account the reputation of the university as well as the price of property. A well-established, well-respected university will continue to attract students, even if there is a long-term downturn in the student intake. Any downturn in student intake is likely to

---

2   Halifax press release, 26 June 2006.

affect universities with a poorer academic reputation. The *Sunday Times Good University Guide* is essential reading if you want to check a university's current rating and how well it is doing year to year.

It is also worth comparing the drop out rate between universities. If a university has a high drop-out rate amongst first year students, that will affect the demand for privately rented properties from second and third year students. If a landlord is letting to first year students it may also affect him or her directly with mid-tenancy voids.

In 2006 the Halifax published a report on house prices in top university towns and found that, in the locations having the top 20 rated universities, those areas that performed best in house price growth over the past five years were Durham (north), Loughborough (east Midlands) and Coventry (west Midlands), closely followed by Leicester (east Midlands). However, as any financial advisor should tell you, past performance is no indication of future performance!

SELECTING THE LOCATION AND TYPE OF PROPERTY

Assuming you have selected the town/city you want to buy your property in, the next thing you need to do is decide which location is best for students. At this point contact the accommodation office at each of the local higher education institutions and get their advice about where students want to live. Of course, you can also contact estate agents and letting agents, but bear in mind that it is in their interest to sell whatever they have lurking on their books and they will not know the student market as well as the institutions themselves.

One sure factor in determining student areas is to find out the routes of public transport to the university sites. In Brighton, for example, popular student areas are those that are a short walk from stops on the number 25 bus route, or close to one of the train stations along the line to Falmer.

Getting a feel for an area

The next thing is to look at the areas along those routes and see how 'student friendly' they feel. Are there plenty of local shops, pubs and takeaways? The 'busier' an area feels, the more likely it is to appeal to students. It may be that those areas along the university bus route which are closer to town are more popular than those which are closer to campus. Students enjoy nightlife and, if they are not living right on the campus, tend to prefer to live closer to the night time action rather than in a suburban area which may be close to the campus, but doesn't feel 'student friendly'.

If you are looking at an area during the first part of an academic year and there are a lot of 'to let' boards, then it is probably an area that is not popular with students. Another good tip is to look at an area in the dark. If it seems dark and threatening then it won't be popular with students. Good street lighting is essential for student security.

What size property?

When it comes to choosing the type of property, much will depend on what you can afford. Most students tend to congregate into groups of four or five, but larger houses that can take bigger groups are also popular and there is always a market for two-bed flats and even studios. If you do buy a leasehold property you will need to get permission from the freeholder before letting it out. It is common for landlords to buy a standard three-bed terrace and convert one of the living rooms into a fourth bedroom, making it a four-bed student let with kitchen, bathroom and communal area.

If you are going for a larger property you must ensure that you have at least one wc and bathroom facility for every five students. You should also ensure you have enough cooking and food storage space. Ideally, you will need to provide more than one fridge-freezer if you have more than four students. You also need to be aware of the impact of HMO licensing on larger properties (see Chapter 3).

DECIDING WHEN TO BUY

Timing is all-important in the student property market. Most students attend university from mid-September to the end of June. Most students do not want to move during an academic year. This means that you should be timing any purchase so that you are ready to let from mid to late September at the latest. You will need to allow around three months for a purchase to go through, plus a little extra for marketing and getting the property ready to let.

On that basis, I would recommend that you start your search for properties from around April and aim to have completion by mid to late August. Leaving it any later than this means it will be difficult to get a group of students in. Completing on a property much earlier, say before the beginning of June, will mean that it is likely to be lying empty for a long period of time.

LETTING PART OF YOUR OWN HOME

If you already live in a university town and have been thinking about letting out part of your own home to students, this is perfectly feasible. On the whole most UK students at university do not want to live in this sort of environment, as part of the experience for them of going to university is living with a whole crowd of other young people. However, there are many international students who really appreciate the home comforts of living in a family environment and perhaps having meals cooked for them as well.

On the whole, unless you are letting to more than two students in your home, you will not have to comply with the raft of legislation detailed elsewhere in this book. You will, however, still need a landlord's gas safety certificate and I would recommend that you get your property checked for electrical safety and install smoke alarms if you do not already have them.

If you let to more than two unrelated people in your own home you will become a **house in multiple occupation** (HMO) and may be licensable as such. Read the section on HMOs in Chapter 3 for details of what you will need to comply with.

As far as tenancy agreements go, you will not be able to issue an assured shorthold tenancy if you are sharing facilities with your tenant. However, I would still recommend that you have a basic agreement in writing, covering such things as how much rent is paid and how often, how much deposit and what it will cover, any house rules and how much notice either side has to give if they want to terminate the agreement.

You will still be able to register with a local university as any other landlord would. You may even find that they have a separate language school as part of the university that will be able to find students for you on a short-term basis at a higher rate.

TAX MATTERS

Unfortunately, once you start making a rental profit on your property, you will have to pay tax. If you are letting out a room in your own home, Her Majesty's Revenue and Customs (HMRC) will allow you to earn up to a certain amount (£4,250 per year in 2007/08) before paying tax, under its 'Rent a Room Scheme'. Letting out a separate property will incur tax on any profit you make. This means that you will need to keep careful records on rent received, your allowable expenses and capital costs for each tax year.

Allowable expenses will reduce your taxable profit, so include as many as you can. Any or all of the following apply:

- Letting agent's, accountant's and legal fees.
- Building and contents insurance.
- Property loan interest (but not any part of the mortgage which is a repayment).
- Maintenance and repairs (but not improvements).
- Utility bills (that you pay, not those the tenant pays!).
- Rent, ground rent and service charges.
- Council tax (again, any that you pay).
- Advertising costs.
- Other direct costs of letting, such as telephone calls.

You can also claim a 10% 'wear and tear' allowance for furnished properties. This means that you can deduct 10% of the gross rent received for the year and class that as an allowable expense.

It is important that you keep your rental business income separate from your personal income so that you can complete your tax return accurately. If you want the tax office to calculate how much tax you need to pay, you will need to send the return in by 30 September following the end of the tax year in April. If you do your own calculations, you have until 31 January. Personally, I recommend completing the tax return on-line (*www.hmrc.gov.uk*) as it does the calculations for you.

There are separate tax rules for landlords who live outside the UK. If this applies to you, and you let your property through a letting agent or university head leasing scheme, they are obliged to deduct tax from your rent before paying you. This rule also applies to your tenants if they are paying you direct, but only if their rent is more than £100 per week. More information on this is available in leaflet IR140 which is available from the tax office.

Capital Gains Tax deserves a brief mention here. If you sell your rental property you will have to pay capital gains tax on the increase in value since you bought it. However, there is some 'taper relief' depending on how long you have owned the property. See the HMRC website for more details on this (www.hmrc.gov.uk). If you used to live in the property yourself as your main home and you sell within three years of moving out, then no capital gains tax is due.

SUMMARY

◆ Work out your finances and consult a financial advisor before proceeding with a purchase.

◆ Calculate relative yields of properties in areas you are interested in.

◆ Decide where in the country you are going to purchase, taking into account capital growth as well as yields.

◆ Talk to the universities and research student areas in the town you have selected to be sure of getting a property that will be popular.

◆ Time your purchase to fit in with the student letting year.

$$\boxed{3}$$

Getting your Property Ready to Let

IN THIS CHAPTER

Houses in multiple occupation

HMO licensing

The Housing, Health and Safety Rating System

Gas and electrical safety checks

Fire safety

Energy efficiency – new rules

Accreditation schemes and codes of standards

Furnishings, décor and facilities

Security

Insurance

As mentioned earlier, letting property involves complying with an increasing amount of legislation. Failure to comply can have severe financial penalties and, in some cases, result in imprisonment. Although the list of things to check and comply with seems quite daunting at first, don't let it put you off – most things are quite easy to implement and, although possibly expensive when you are first converting a property for letting, not overly onerous once the initial work is done.

Apart from the safety checks and legislative standards required, you also need to ensure that you equip and secure your property adequately for letting to students.

HOUSES IN MULTIPLE OCCUPATION

A House in Multiple Occupation (HMO) is defined by Sections 254–259 of the Housing Act 2004. It applies to any property with living accommodation where amenities are shared by two or more households. A household is defined as people who are the same family, which includes couples living together. Managers of HMOs have to comply with certain standards in order to let their accommodation and may, in some circumstances, have to be licensed with the local authority (see next section).

There are some exemptions to the definition of an HMO, which include the following.

◆ Properties which are predominantly owner-occupied, including a resident landlord (and their family) who does not share accommodation with more than two other unrelated people.

♦ Properties which are occupied by only two unrelated people, e.g. a flat occupied by two friends.

The other exemptions are not normally relevant to a private sector landlord letting in the student market. There are also separate rules if the building you own is a block of flats. For example, if you own a block of converted flats where at least 2/3rds are owner occupied, then the building would not be classed as an HMO. However, if the flat you rent out in that building is let to three or more people, then that flat would become an HMO (or, to be more accurate, a Flat in Multiple Occupation).

You should assume that, if you are letting a property in England to more than two students (who are not in the same family) and they are sharing amenities then you are operating an HMO and will need to comply with the Management of Houses in Multiple Occupation (England) Regulations 2006. In essence, these require you to do the following.

♦ Ensure your name, address and telephone contact number are supplied and clearly displayed in the property.

♦ Ensure that means of escape from fire are kept free from obstruction and kept in good repair.

♦ Ensure that fire fighting equipment and alarms are kept in good order and repair.

♦ Take all measures reasonably required to protect the occupiers from injury.

- Ensure that the water supply and drainage system are in good, clean and working condition and not unreasonably allow the water supply to be interrupted.

- Provide a gas appliance test certificate to the local authority if requested.

- Ensure that electrical inspections are carried out at least every five years.

- Maintain common parts and common fixtures, fittings and appliances.

- Ensure that outbuildings, gardens, yards, forecourts as well as boundary walls, fences and railings are kept in good and safe repair.

- Ensure that each unit of living accommodation is clean at the beginning of a person's occupation of it and is subsequently maintained in good repair.

- Ensure that there are sufficient bins or other refuse receptacles for the occupants and arrange for disposal of refuse and litter, having regard to services provided by the local authority.

As you can see, the requirements are not onerous and are what any reasonable landlord would do (or arrange to be done) as a normal part of their role as a property manager.

HMO LICENSING

If your property is to be let to five or more tenants *and* it is on three or more storeys then it will become subject to mandatory licensing with the local authority. Licensing will incur a fee, which varies widely according to which local authority your property is in. The average fee is around £500 (the licence lasts for five years), but the fee in some areas is approaching £2,000.

Being licensable means that you have to meet higher standards of safety, management and amenities within your property. The exact requirements have, on the whole, been left to be decided by local authorities, but are likely to include the provision of fire safety measures such as mains-linked fire alarms, emergency lighting, fire doors on each room and heat detectors in cooking areas as well as a specified level of provision of bathrooms, WCs, kitchens, laundry facilities and equipment.

Controversially, national legislation has required that each unit of living accommodation (i.e. bedroom) has to have a wash hand-basin. Sensibly, most local authorities are stipulating that a landlord has up to five years to comply with this clause. It is possible that this clause will be quietly dropped in any review of the legislation as it has caused a loud outcry from landlords and local authorities alike.

If your property is licensable it is important that you apply to the local authority for a licence. Failure to do so is a criminal offence and can incur a fine of up to £20,000. It may also mean that your tenants are not liable to pay you rent for any period in which you remain unlicensed.

As well as mandatory licensing, local authorities can introduce selective licensing if they feel that it is necessary. So even if you are not letting a property to five or more tenants on three or more storeys, you need to check with the local authority that your property does not need to be licensed under a selective scheme.

THE HOUSING, HEALTH AND SAFETY RATING SYSTEM (HHSRS)

HHSRS was also introduced by the Housing Act 2004 and applies to all properties in England and Wales – even owner-occupied ones! It is a method for assessing the health and safety of a residential dwelling and replaces the old-fashioned 'fitness standard' that was assessed and implemented by local authority environmental health officers (EHOs). As a landlord, it is important for you to be aware of the general theory as your property could be assessed by an EHO at any time as part of licensing or in response to a complaint from your tenants.

There are 29 'hazards' to be assessed, which fall into four main areas as shown opposite.

For each hazard there are two possible judgements, which are:

- the likelihood, over the next 12 months, of an occurrence that could result in harm to a 'vulnerable occupier'; and

- the range of potential harm outcomes from such an occurrence to a 'vulnerable occupier', from extreme harm such as death through to serious illness or conditions, down to minor health problems.

The calculation of the category of hazard is complicated and we will not go into detail here. It is sufficient to know that if an EHO

Physiological requirements	Psychological requirements	Protection from infection	Protection from accidents
Excess cold	Crowding and space	Domestic hygiene, pests and refuse	Falls associated with baths
Damp and mould	Entry by intruders	Food safety	Falls on level services
Excess heat	Lighting	Personal hygiene and drainage	Falls on stairs
Asbestos	Noise	Water supply	Falls between levels
Biocides			Electrical hazards
Carbon monoxide			Fire
Lead			Flames and hot surfaces
Radiation			Collision and entrapment
Uncombusted fuel gas			Position and operability of amenities
Volatile organic compounds			Explosions
			Structural collapse and falling elements

found a Category 1 hazard the local authority has a duty to take enforcement action against a landlord. If there is a Category 2 hazard there is a power to take action, but no duty. Whether or not action is enforceable will depend, in part, on the current occupants. For example, a tripping hazard will be more dangerous to an elderly occupant than it would be to a group of students.

GAS AND ELECTRICAL SAFETY CHECKS

There are two main checks that must be undertaken by law before you are able to let out your property. Copies of both certificates should be given to your tenants and the university you are registered with will probably also require copies before advertising your property.

1. Gas safety

We have all heard of the dangers of carbon monoxide poisoning. A few years ago students were regularly victims of poorly maintained gas appliances and many lost their lives as a result. More recently we hear of deaths in Mediterranean holiday resorts caused by dangerous gas appliances.

Under the Gas Safety (Installation and Use) Regulations 1998 a landlord is required to ensure that all gas installations and appliances are maintained in good working order. Annual safety checks of gas appliances, fittings and flues must be carried out by a CORGI (Council for Registered Gas Installers) registered gas engineer who will then provide you with a landlord's gas safety certificate. The checks must be carried out within the year before the tenancy begins. Copies of the safety check must be given to each tenant within 28 days of them moving in and a record of the test must be kept for two years. Any equipment failing a safety test must be repaired by a CORGI registered gas installer before it can be used again. The landlord also has a duty to ensure that tenants are aware of their obligations under the Regulations.

Further information on gas safety can be obtained from the Health and Safety Executive (tel: 0800 300 363) and useful leaflets for your tenants informing them on their rights and responsibilities under the legislation can be ordered free from CORGI.

2. Electrical safety

All HMOs are now required to have an electrical safety certificate confirming the property has been inspected and found safe by an electrician who is registered with a relevant body, such as the NICEIC (National Inspection Council for Electrical Installation Contracting). The enforcing body for HMO regulations is the local council where the property is situated and most authorities will require this certificate to be updated every five years. However, check with your local council to ensure that this is the case for you. You will almost certainly have to provide a copy of the electrical safety certificate to a university if you wish to register with them as a landlord.

FIRE SAFETY

If you are operating an HMO you are now required to undertake a risk assessment of the level of fire safety provision, determine a fire escape route and act accordingly. Recent fire safety legislation (Regulatory Reform (Fire Safety) Order 2005) applies to the common areas of HMOs and the guidance issues requires landlords of such properties to comply with a high level of fire safety provision. This new legislation is mostly aimed at non-domestic premises but, unfortunately, does apply to 'sleeping accommodation' where it falls within the definition of an HMO. The Fire Service is the body which enforces the rules and, at the time of writing, many local fire officers are more concerned with the enforcement of the rules in large premises such as hostels, student halls of residence, blocks of flats, etc, rather than in small shared houses of the type you are probably managing. However, in light of the new rules, I would recommend that you contact the local council where your property is located and ask them for guidance on what fire safety provisions they require an HMO to have and be prepared for any or all of the following to be required:

- A fire blanket complying with BS 1869 which should be firmly fixed in the kitchen (but not above the cooker as the occupiers will not them be able to reach for it in the event of a cooker fire!).

- A mains wired inter-linked fire alarm system covering each floor of the property with a heat detector in the kitchen.

- Fire doors of minimum 30 minute fire resistance rating, with hydraulic self closures) on each room opening onto a fire escape route (which is normally the staircase, corridors and hallway).

- A fire extinguisher on each floor of the property.

- Check all fire equipment and alarm systems regularly.

You also need to give your tenants fire safety information and check that they are not misusing equipment provided. (Common practices are wedging open fire doors, taking batteries out of smoke detectors or putting socks over heat detectors!)

In addition to the general measures above, you will need to ensure that any upholstered furnishings you provide comply with the Furniture and Furnishings (Fire Safety) Regulations 1988, as amended in 1989 and 1993. All such furniture is required to carry a permanent label giving information about its fire retardant properties. The furniture the regulations apply to include the following.

- Beds – including bases, mattresses and upholstered headboards.
- Futons and sofabeds.
- Sofas and armchairs.
- Cushions and pillows.
- Dining chairs, if they include any upholstering.
- Outdoor upholstered furniture if it could be used indoors.
- Stretch, loose and fitted coverings for furniture.

The regulations, however, do not apply to items such as sleeping bags, pillowcases, duvets, mattress covers, curtains, carpets or any furniture manufactured before 1950.

Before letting your property double check that all relevant furniture displays one of the labels. If it doesn't, replace it.

ENERGY EFFICIENCY – NEW RULES

From August 2007 the government is introducing Home Information Packs in England and Wales for properties having four bedrooms or more, which means that anyone selling such a property must provide potential buyers with a pack. Every pack will include an Energy Performance Certificate and it is envisaged that such certificates will need to be provided for any property being sold or let from October 2008.

An Energy Performance Certificate will provide future purchasers and tenants with A-G ratings (similar to fridge ratings) on the property they will be renting as well as a list of practical measures to cut their fuel bills and carbon emissions. A highly rated property is likely to be more attractive to a group of student tenants as it will mean they are less likely to spend money on heating costs.

It is, therefore, worth bearing in mind what measures you, as a landlord, can put in place now, to ensure that your property is rated well when the legislation comes into force.

ACCREDITATION SCHEMES AND CODES OF STANDARDS

You may find that, in order to register with a university to offer accommodation to students, you need to sign up to either an accreditation scheme or a code of standards. The main difference between the two is that accreditation schemes should be voluntary and are offered as a way of distinguishing your property as being more safe and secure (with possibly more amenities) than other properties being offered. Codes of standards, however, are usually compulsory and are a set of minimum standards that you need to provide in order to register with a particular institution.

Such schemes were introduced in the early 1990s because student accommodation was notoriously poor in quality and safety. At the time there was little legislation to ensure that properties were safe and institutions felt that they needed to offer their students some sort of level of safety in the private rented sector after they had moved out of halls of residence. Gradually, local authorities also came on board and the government became interested in this voluntary initiative which was springing up to meet a gap in legislation. Local authorities now get central government funds for running and promoting such schemes.

What the schemes cover

All schemes will cover physical standards in a property, such as fire safety provision, energy efficiency, security etc, but also will have management standards such as providing fair and proper contracts, timescales for repairs and return of deposits, and provision of clear information. Schemes will vary as to whether they accredit the landlord (and therefore all their properties have to comply) or whether they accredit the property (and therefore not all properties have to comply). Schemes also vary widely as to whether they ask for a 'reasonable' standard or go for something over and above that.

Whether such schemes have much merit these days is now debatable as there is a plethora of legislation (as this chapter demonstrates) which applies to the private rented sector. However, such university schemes are often linked to a local council accreditation scheme which may offer benefits and discounts with local suppliers. Universities themselves may undertake to market your properties to students more forcefully if you are accredited. If the scheme is voluntary it can demonstrate to your potential tenants that you are offering them a decent standard of accommodation and are a landlord to be trusted.

Deciding whether to join a scheme

Unipol, a charitable student accommodation provider in Leeds, offer a voluntary Code of Standards to landlords and find that 80% of their landlords join because of the benefits they can get through the scheme. A survey of their student customers indicated that 77% thought it was important to rent a property from a landlord who was signed up to the Code of Standards.

Whether you decide to join one will inevitably depend on: whether it is compulsory in order for you to let to students or, if voluntary, whether the benefits to you outweigh the effort required to meet the standard, or if you feel morally obliged to join such a scheme.

FURNISHINGS, DECOR AND FACILITIES

Although there are some mature students who may wish to rent an unfurnished property it is usually the case that students expect their rented properties to be fully furnished. A suggested inventory is provided at the back of the book as Appendix 1. In brief, though, the usual white goods should be supplied in the kitchen – cooker, fridge-freezer (one for every four tenants preferably), and possibly a washing machine. Many landlords, however, choose not to supply a washing machine as students are notoriously prone to damaging them by over-loading with towels and wrenching doors open before the locking mechanism has disengaged. An alternative plan is to supply the plumbing connection for a washing machine and let the tenants rent one themselves (or use a launderette).

It is not necessary to supply items such as kettles, microwaves or irons – tenants can bring their own and then you are not responsible for keeping them in working order.

The usual furniture in other areas should be supplied – a table and chairs for eating meals, a sofa and/or easy chairs for relaxing in the communal living room. Each bedroom should be equipped for studying as well as sleeping – so supply a desk, bookshelves and desk chair as well as the usual bed (double beds are preferred if the room is large enough), wardrobe and chest of drawers.

Although it is tempting to go for new flat pack furniture from places such as Argos and Ikea, I recommend that you spend a little more and either go for higher quality self-assemble furniture or buy good quality, sturdy secondhand furniture. Firstly, you won't have to assemble it and secondly, it usually lasts longer under the strain of heavy student use. It is also a good idea to provide mattress protectors – you will probably have to replace them each year, but it's better than having stained mattresses.

Bathrooms should definitely have a shower, although a bath is not necessary. Any toilet in the property should have a wash-hand basin close by.

What you should provide

Do not provide items such as crockery, cutlery, cooking pans, vases, pictures or other paraphernalia you would expect in your own home. Students are used to bringing these items themselves when they move into a hall of residence and it is just a waste of your time to count up and charge for any such items that go missing during a tenancy. I would suggest, however, that you provide cleaning equipment such as mops, buckets, bins, dustpan and brush, if only to encourage your tenants to keep the property clean. Expect to have to replace most of these items each year and it really isn't worth claiming for them from the deposit when you can buy most of them for around £2 each. You will also need to provide a vacuum cleaner that you should get serviced each year between tenancies.

If your property has a garden and you expect the tenants to maintain it, make sure they have the correct equipment to do so.

Case Study

Mr S

Mr S rented out a five-bed property to a group of students and lodged the deposit with an independent third party deposit holder. At the end of the tenancy he made a claim on the deposit for cleaning as well as the replacement of several minor items, including: a duster, a vase, two teaspoons and a mop.

He was most annoyed when the dispute went to arbitration and, although awarded some costs for cleaning, was not awarded money for the replacement of what the arbitration panel considered to be 'minor items which would have to be replaced from time to time'. The panel recommended that he should not provide such a large amount of small items to his student tenants in the future. ■

Preventing damp damage

Because of the high number of adults in most student properties and their tendency to bath/shower and cook individually and at frequent intervals, I would recommend that you fit a good extractor fan in both the kitchen and bathroom. If not, you may find that condensation mould builds up on cold exterior walls as the high level of humidity condenses in houses that are heated in accordance with a student budget.

For the same reason make sure you let students know that they should not dry their washing by draping it over radiators. Provide them with an airer they can put in a warm room if the weather is not good enough to hang washing out on a line which you should also provide.

Décor

The décor of student houses varies enormously. Landlords who have been letting for a long time tend to favour the swirly carpet look which is often accompanied by patterned wallpaper from circa 1978. However, students are as swayed by the current rash of property makeover programmes as anyone else and, if you can, providing laminate flooring and plain painted walls will look much more attractive and date far more slowly. Laminate flooring is also easier to keep clean and it doesn't suffer from the rash of coffee and red wine stains that student carpets tend to endure.

Hang good quality curtains or blinds at the windows. Fragile fittings will only fall off fairly rapidly as young adults tend to be more vigorous in their movements than more sedate occupants.

SECURITY

Student properties are often, unfortunately, the target of the local burglar population. The lure of multiple laptops, I-pods and other technical gadgetry makes a student home likely to offer a good haul. Ensure that external doors to the property are of solid construction and have good five-lever mortise locks. Basement and ground floor windows should have locks. If your property has been burgled in the past it may be worth fitting a burglar alarm.

In some areas it is possible for student tenants to get funding from the local police to install security measures. If you are lucky enough to have a property in an area which benefits from this, make the most of it!

INSURANCE

You will, of course, need to insure your property. You will not be able to use a normal domestic insurance policy for rented properties and I recommend that you contact the landlord associations listed in the Appendix at the back of this book to find the most competitive deal for the type of property you let out. If you belong to a landlord association, or a local accreditation scheme, you will probably get a discount. Most landlords tend to go for buildings only insurance, and do not bother with the contents. However, if you have expensive, sturdy, well-maintained furniture, then it is worth getting that covered too. It is also worth noting that you can get insurance policies that will cover you for loss of rent if major disrepair happens to your property and your tenants have to move out temporarily.

Any insurance policy you do get will cover your property only, not the students' belongings. Remind them that they need to get their own contents cover.

SUMMARY

◆ Ensure you comply with HMO standards.

◆ Check if your property needs to be licensed with the local authority for the area.

◆ Get a landlord's gas safety certificate from a CORGI registered gas engineer.

◆ Get an electrical safety certificate from a properly qualified electrician.

- Provide adequate fire safety measures, including fire resistant soft furnishings.

- Make the property secure from criminals and get it properly insured.

- Provide extractor fans in the bathroom and kitchen.

- Decorate in neutral, easy to clean wall and floor coverings.

- Provide good quality furniture and articles, but don't go overboard with minor household items.

- If there is a local accreditation scheme, join it to enjoy the benefits and gain recognition for the high standard of your property.

Tenancy Agreements

IN THIS CHAPTER

What is a tenancy?

Tenancy v licence

Assured Shorthold Tenancies

Non-assured tenancies

Joint tenancies

Tenancies for leasehold properties

Unfair terms

Distance selling regulations

Future changes

Getting advice

WHAT IS A TENANCY?

A tenancy is a type of contract concerning the temporary ownership of land. An often forgotten fact is that it does not have to be in writing – although any legal advisor would recommend that it was, so that both parties are clear on their rights and obligations and, if it should ever become a dispute in court, that the court can also see what was agreed by the parties. In addition, if your tenant requests it, you are obliged to provide a statement of the main terms within 28 days. So you might as well have a written tenancy agreement from the beginning.

Tenancies are a type of contract, but incorporate some of the ancient customs of land law. Short term tenancies (less than seven years) fall within a branch of law known as housing law – which is a small and largely unrewarding part of law for most solicitors. There are solicitors who specialise in housing law but, although the law is complex, I would advise that you acquaint yourself with the main facts I set out in this chapter. Fortunately there are plenty of 'off the shelf' tenancy agreements available at high street shops or from the internet, so there is no need for a landlord to engage a solicitor for drafting a tenancy agreement.

Because tenancies concern the living arrangements of a high percentage of people (approximately 12% nationally) they are subject to a high volume of central government legislation, the primary function of which is to protect a largely vulnerable section of the population from the worst excesses of Rachman-like landlords. Because of this some landlords have tried to let property in a way that circumvents tenancy law by issuing a licence instead.

TENANCY v LICENCE

A licence is not a tenancy agreement. A licence is essentially a right to be somewhere or to do something. It stops an occupier of a property from being a trespasser, but it does not give as many rights as a tenancy. The crucial difference between a tenancy and a licence is that the former offers 'exclusive possession' of a room or property – meaning that the tenant has the right to exclude the landlord (or anyone else). A tenancy also has a right to repair under the Landlord and Tenant Act 1985 implied into the agreement and it will also be more difficult to evict a tenant than a licensee.

Some of you may now be thinking that issuing licences instead of tenancies is a good idea! However, even if you call your agreement a licence, if the occupier can be found to have exclusive possession of whatever they are occupying a court will still imply the rights and responsibilities of a tenancy agreement into the so-called licence (or 'sham' tenancy).

Issuing a licence

The main instance where you would issue a licence rather than a tenancy is if you were letting a room in your own home and were providing services such as meals or cleaning. In such a case you would only need to give 'reasonable notice' in order to evict an occupier. Reasonable notice would normally be whatever the rental period is, but should be no less than two weeks.

Another example of how a licence operates might be where you are letting out a house to several individuals, giving them each tenancy agreements for their own rooms. In such a case they would have a tenancy for their own room and, by necessity, a licence to use the communal areas. The main advantage of this for you is that they do not have exclusive possession of the communal areas and, therefore, you have the right to enter the communal areas without giving the 24 hours' notice that would be required under a tenancy. However, the drawback is that you do not have the greater security of several tenants being liable to you under a joint tenancy (see below).

ASSURED SHORTHOLD TENANCIES

In most cases, where you are letting out a separate property from the one you live in, you will be issuing an Assured Shorthold Tenancy (AST). Assured tenancies were brought in by the Housing Act 1988 and revolutionised the letting market. Prior to this legislation landlords let properties and were never sure when they would be getting them back again. The phenomenon of 'sitting tenants' still haunts the nightmares of long-term landlords and frustrated property developers.

The introduction of Assured and Assured Shorthold Tenancies meant that landlords were better able to control when they got their properties back. The Housing Act 1996 amended this to make ASTs the default tenancy so now, apart from some intended exceptions, any private sector tenancy issued since 28 February 1997 is an AST. It is very easy to obtain pre-drafted AST agreements from high street stationers and on the internet.

How ASTs work

An AST guarantees your tenants security of tenure in the property for a minimum of six months. If you issue a fixed term tenancy (i.e. a tenancy for a stated period of time) for longer than six months then, unless you have reserved the right to give notice after six months, they will be guaranteed security of tenure for whatever period you have stated (unless they breach their side of the agreement).

In the student letting market you will normally be issuing a tenancy for a minimum of nine months, or even up to 12 months. You can, of course, try to insist on only six months, but most students will go elsewhere. If you do find a group wanting a property for only six months they will leave in March and you will then have trouble letting the property to another group of students – most of whom will be tied into a tenancy until June or July at least.

To be sure of bringing a fixed term AST to an end you must issue a Section 21 Notice Seeking Possession at least two months before the end of a fixed term. If you do not do this then your tenants can stay on after the end of the term of the tenancy until you have obtained a court order for repossession, which may take some time. This will cause problems for whomever you have agreed to let to for the following academic year. If you all agree to continue the tenancy, however, you can choose to issue another fixed term tenancy or allow the current tenancy to continue on its existing terms, in which case it becomes a 'periodic' tenancy. A periodic tenancy can be ended by either party – the landlord has to give two months' or eight weeks' notice (depending on whether the rent is paid monthly or weekly) or the tenant has to give one month's or four weeks' notice.

Periodic tenancies
You can choose to issue your tenants with an AST that does not have a fixed term, but runs from month to month (or week to

week) until brought to an end by one of the parties. I do not recommend you do this (although I am always delighted for students who have a problem landlord and have been given this type of tenancy!).

Basically it means that your tenants can move out at any time by giving notice of either one month or four weeks (depending on the rental period). In theory you can give them notice of either two months or eight weeks. However, no court will enforce this until six months of the tenancy have elapsed. This puts you at an unfair disadvantage if you do wish to evict your tenants.

NON-ASSURED TENANCIES

There are some instances where private sector tenancies are not assured. One example is a tenancy where the annual rent comes to more than £25,000. Another example is where a landlord lets out a separate flat in a building that he occupies. For example, you may live in a three-storey house that has a converted self-contained flat in the basement, which you let out to a couple. As such you are a residential landlord and therefore excluded from the Housing Acts 1988 and 1996. You would be issuing an 'excluded tenancy'. Your tenants would still have a better security of tenure than if they were sharing your living accommodation as you would have to issue a four-week Notice to Quit if you wanted them to move out and follow this up with a court order if they failed to go.

If you live in a purpose-built block of flats and are letting out another flat in the same block, you will be issuing an AST as purpose built flats are covered by the relevant Acts.

JOINT TENANCIES

You can choose to issue your tenants with individual tenancies for their rooms, but I wouldn't recommend it. It does mean that you have greater control over the common areas of the property, but there are more advantages to issuing a joint tenancy. A possible problem with issuing individual tenancies to a group of tenants is that a court may hold the tenancy to be joint anyway, particularly if the group of tenants share all facilities, and shop and pay bills between them.

A joint tenancy usually means that a group of people occupying a property all sign one tenancy between them. This means that they are jointly and severally liable for their side of the agreement. In other words, if one of them defaults on the rent and disappears you can recover the rent from any one of the other tenants (presumably the one with the most expensive-looking car). Likewise, if one of them trashes the house you can use the deposit from all of them to cover the damage.

There is one slight contradiction to the above. In law no more than four individuals can hold a legal interest in the same piece of land (s34 Trustee Act 1925). If, therefore, you issue a joint tenancy agreement to five students, the first four named hold the legal interest on trust for themselves and the fifth. If you do have to take the group to court for a breach of their tenancy, you can only sue the first four named on the agreement. In practice this doesn't really matter to you (although it does to the four named tenants if it's the fifth who has defaulted!) as they are still liable for any breaches of the agreement. You might, however, kick yourself rather hard if the bailiffs are unable to recover any valuable possessions from the first four tenants and the fifth is sunning herself on her parents' yacht!

Case Study

Mr F

Mr F let his property to a group of four second-year students. Two months after the tenancy commenced Anna, one of the group, rang him to say that she was dropping out of her course and returning to her family home 200 miles away. Mr F pointed out her liability under the tenancy i.e. that she was still obliged to pay the rent. Anna said that he could keep her deposit, but she was not prepared to pay any more in rent and that he would have to look to the other members of the household.

Mr F contacted the university for advice and was told that they would re-advertise the empty room to help him fill the vacancy as soon as possible. They also advised him to write to the remaining tenants stating that he would be expecting them to pay the extra rent if a new tenant was not found by the time Anna's deposit ran out. This had the advantage of ensuring that the tenants were not obstructive about room viewings or about who was introduced as a replacement. It also reminded them of their responsibilities under the tenancy.

Fortunately the property was in good condition and in a popular area so another tenant was found fairly quickly. However, if rent arrears had started to build up, Mr F could have chosen to either pursue Anna for the remaining rent, or any or all of the other tenants because of the joint and several liability of the tenancy they were bound by. ◼

If you have issued a periodic tenancy, or the existing fixed term has become a periodic tenancy (or has a clause which enables the tenants to bring the tenancy to an end), it is important to bear in mind that, if one of your joint tenants gives notice which you accept, it will bring the entire tenancy to an end, even if the other tenants do not agree. Although, if you want them to stay on, you can just issue a new tenancy to the remaining tenants and whomever else they bring in to replace the one leaving.

TENANCIES FOR LEASEHOLD PROPERTIES
If you are letting a property which is already subject to a long lease, e.g. in a block of flats, it is important to ensure that any terms which you are required to observe as part of the lease are included in the tenancy agreement you issue to your tenants.

For example, a term in the lease forbidding the hanging of washing outside must be reflected in the tenancy you issue, otherwise your tenants may cause you to be in breach of the superior lease.

UNFAIR TERMS
The Unfair Terms in Consumer Contracts Regulations (UTCCR) 1999 applies to tenancy contracts that have not been individually negotiated (i.e. they are in a 'standard form') and are between a business and consumer. In this context landlords are operating as business. Essentially the Office of Fair Trading (OFT), which provides guidance on this area, states that you must ensure that the terms in your contracts:

♦ are transparent and in good faith
♦ do not create a significant imbalance to the consumer's detriment
♦ are in plain intelligible language.

Examples of terms which would fail the OFT test are as follows.

- Anything that includes 'legalese' such as 'notwithstanding as hereinbefore recited'.

- Terms that bind your tenants to go on paying for a service that is not provided as agreed.

- Terms which require your tenant to insure with a particular insurer.

- Misleading termination clauses, e.g. stating that the landlord has the right to re-enter the property if the tenant is more than seven days late paying the rent *without* informing the tenant that the landlord has to have a court order first.

- Terms that forbid your tenant from subletting (better to say they can 'sublet with permission, such permission not to be unreasonably withheld').

- Terms that forbid animals (better to say 'animals which are likely to cause damage').

Standard letting agreements such as those produced by Oyez now take into account what is required under this area of legislation, but the law is constantly changing. If a term of your agreement was found to be unfair it is not enforceable against the tenant. However, you will be reassured to know that 'core' terms such as the amount of rent charged, the length of the tenancy, etc are exempt from UTCCR requirements.

There is a useful leaflet produced by the OFT called 'Unfair tenancy terms: don't get caught out' which is available on the OFT website at www.oft.gov.uk

DISTANCE SELLING REGULATIONS

For most small landlords dealing face to face with their tenants, this section will not apply. But, just in case you find yourself concluding a contract with tenants you have not yet met (e.g. by email, post, on-line, fax, telephone), bear the following points in mind.

The Consumer Protection (Distance Selling) Regulations 2005 apply to:

◆ contracts between a supplier and consumer
◆ where the supplier is dealing in the course of a business, and
◆ there is exclusive use of one or more types of distance communication.

The regulations come into force at the point the contract is formed if the supplier has not met the consumer before this point. The effect of the regulations is to give the consumer (your tenant) cancellation rights any time up to three months and seven working days after the contract is formed – which could cause you serious problems. Providing accommodation does allow you to benefit from some exclusions, however. You can state that the right to cancel does not apply once the tenants have moved into the property.

If you find yourself in the position of falling within distance selling rules, these are the best ways to protect yourself.

- Decide and state when your contract is formed (e.g. 'this contract comes into force when it has been signed and dated by both parties').

- Decide what the cancellation period will be (there has to be one in distance selling and it must be a minimum of seven days from when the contract is formed) and state it as part of the application procedure.

- Quote the regulations when stating the cancellation period.

- Make it clear that the right to cancel does not apply once the tenants have taken up occupation (as an accommodation provider you can benefit from this exception to the general distance selling rules).

An ideal clause to add into your contract is:

This Agreement comes into force when it has been signed and dated by the Landlord and the Tenant and the tenancy begins at the start of the Tenancy Period. Where the Consumer Protection (Distance Selling) Regulations 2005 apply, the Tenant may cancel the agreement within seven days after the Agreement comes into force. The right to cancel does not apply after the start of the Tenancy Period.

FUTURE CHANGES

Even lawyers admit that housing law is complex and confusing. The government has recognised that the whole area needs to be consolidated and rationalised. To this end the Law Commission has recommended a complete change to the existing tenure system and, in May 2006, released a draft Rented Homes Bill for government to implement.

The main proposals are these.

◆ To replace all existing tenancy types (apart from a few minor exceptions) with just two – the **secure contract**, which would be used by local authorities and housing associations, and the **standard contract**, which would be used by everyone else.

◆ A **model contract** will be provided which landlords can choose to use, and which will comply with the Unfair Terms in Consumer Contracts Regulations 1999.

◆ A landlord will be able to obtain a possession order on a 'no-fault' basis within the first six months of a standard contract if they have given the correct notice.

◆ The existing long list of grounds of possession will be reduced to just two – breach of the occupation contract and estate management grounds. Standard contracts will also have available the 'notice-only' ground and a mandatory serious rent arrears ground.

◆ The tenant will also have the ability to bring the contract to an end by serving the correct notice.

◆ In possession proceedings the courts will have to be more consistent – a judge will have a checklist of questions he or she must answer before coming to a decision.

The main exceptions to the new tenancy system will continue to include landlords who share their living accommodation with a lodger.

At the time of writing the draft Bill is not listed for immediate consideration by Parliament. The Department for Community and Local Government (DCLG) may, however, publish it during the current session for pre-legislative scrutiny. The earliest it could realistically be presented to Parliament would be 2007/08 with possible enactment in 2008 and reforms coming into force in 2009 or 2010. If the DCLG give it a low priority in the meantime, however, the Law Commission have recommended that the Welsh Assembly should seek powers to legislate for Wales only. In this event it is possible that new tenancy laws could come into force in Wales earlier than in England.

GETTING ADVICE

If, having read through this chapter, you are still unclear about how to go about issuing a tenancy agreement in your particular circumstances, I would recommend that you join a professional landlord organisation as they are a source of usually excellent advice, support and up-to-date information. Contact details of the various organisations are listed at the back of this book.

SUMMARY

- ◆ Ensure you know what type of written agreement you need and check it for potentially unfair terms.

- ◆ Let for a fixed term, rather than periodic, if you want the security of knowing your tenants are bound for a certain length of time.

- If you are letting to more than one tenant in a property do it on a joint tenancy, unless you specifically want individual tenancies.

- If you are concluding a contract without meeting face to face protect yourself against the effects of distance selling regulations.

- Join a professional landlord organisation and get advice and up-to-date information.

Advertising Your Property

IN THIS CHAPTER

Timing

Registering with the university

House-hunting days

Head leasing schemes

Letting/management agents

On-line databases

Advertising your property is one of the most important parts of being in the letting business. Choosing when, where and whom to advertise to starts the process of handing over your investment to people who will hopefully treat it with respect, and reward your hard work and risk with a satisfactory financial return. Getting it wrong at this stage could result in void periods, disorganised tenants and financial expenditure that need not have happened. Make sure you read this chapter and the next before you advertise.

TIMING

Advertising your property to students at the right time will ensure that you get the pick of the best organised and most fully informed tenants and will leave you with the security of knowing that you have your property let for up to the next 18 months (still six months left to run on the current tenancy, plus a group signed up for the following year).

Although it varies slightly from town to town, most students start to think about where they are going to be living for the next academic year when they come back from their Christmas vacation. At this stage they will be eyeing up their current flatmates or course colleagues and trying to decide whether they could bear to spend another 18 months coping with their dubious culinary skills and questionable social habits. They will be making use of the on-line message boards most universities have to get together their 'dream team' of ideal flatmates.

Some universities start contacting their registered landlords (see section below) as early as December to find out what they will have available from the following summer. Many universities leave it to February/March before doing their mail-out to registered landlords. Either way, you need to ensure that you know whether or not you want to keep your existing tenants (assuming they want to stay) or whether you are going to be looking for a new group.

The best times to advertise

Assuming you are looking for a new group, you need to decide if you are going to advertise at the time that current students start to look (between January–April, depending on the university) or whether you are going to leave it to the summer before advertising. There are pros and cons with either method.

Advertising between January and April

Advertising in the January–April period ensures that you get the best choice of well-organised groups of returning undergraduates. They will have selected who they want to live with and have probably been organised enough to attend the university's own housing advice sessions. However, assuming you have chosen a property in the right area and with the right facilities, you will be inundated with calls/emails from students for several days, possibly weeks (absolute heaven for most landlords).

Personally, knowing that I have popular, well-managed properties and am well placed to let them to a good group, I prefer to advertise my properties when the rush dies down a bit in the summer term. However, particularly for new or less experienced landlords, I would recommend that you advertise your property when the universities you are dealing with contact you to ask what you have available for the next academic year.

Advertising in summer

Advertising in the summer term, or summer vacation, ensures that you can take advantage of any 'house-hunting' days (see below) that the university might be running for new students and means that you also have the best chance of securing groups of postgraduates, who bring the advantages of greater maturity, greater desire to work and a diminished desire to party. The disadvantage of this method is that there is always a smaller pool of postgraduates than of undergraduates and you will also be attracting returning students who weren't organised enough to get their group together for the main spring rush and who may, therefore, not be organised enough with their finances either.

Advertising in autumn

If you leave it too late (say, September) you will be attracting incoming first year undergraduates who were too late to be housed by the university. This is fairly disastrous in letting terms as they are unlikely to have lived away from home before (and therefore have no idea how to operate a vacuum cleaner), have over-anxious parents who, at best, will view you with suspicion, and they will be choosing to live in a house, on a joint tenancy, with people they have met approximately ten minutes before coming to view your property. You can almost guarantee that your tenant management skills are going to be put fully to the test.

REGISTERING WITH THE UNIVERSITY

If there's one thing I'd really like to get across in this book, it is that the institutions supplying your prospective tenants offer a wealth of free expert advice and information which you will find useful throughout your life as a landlord letting to students. In some cities, such as Leeds, Manchester and Liverpool, local universities have 'contracted out' their private sector accommodation service to separate organisations (Unipol Student Homes, Manchester Student Homes or Liverpool Student Homes) which handle it all for them and also often provide a management service to landlords as well.

Either way, you should by now have identified the individual in the accommodation office or other student organisation responsible for liasing with and cultivating local landlords. If not, do it now. She/he may well become a valuable source of information about the local letting market and, at the very least, will encourage you to register your property with their university. This entails several benefits to you.

♦ You will get a free booklet (of varying quality and usefulness) informing you of your responsibilities and the requirements of registering with that particular institution as well as a number of useful tips.

♦ If there is a head leasing scheme (see below) you will be informed of the benefits of joining it.

♦ You will be contacted by the university about a month before they start listing private sector properties to students for the next academic year, asking you what you will have available and when you would like to advertise it.

♦ You will be contacted with details of any 'house-hunting' days they organise (see below).

♦ You will be sent updates of useful information from the local council, landlord organisation, etc via the accommodation office.

- ◆ You may be able to use standard tenancy agreement, guarantor forms, etc supplied by the institution.

- ◆ Your property may be visited by an accommodation officer who will certainly be looking for any possible problems, but will also be a useful source of advice about what works well and what doesn't in your particular property.

- ◆ If you do end up having problems with your tenants you can get free advice on what to do and the accommodation officer may also intervene directly if your tenants are doing something that could bring the university into disrepute (e.g. causing a noise nuisance).

Registering with the university may be free of charge or it may involve an annual fee – currently, a typical registration fee is around £25 per property per year. If you have several properties the fee is usually tailored to allow for 'bulk discounts', e.g. three properties registered for £50 per year. Normally this registration fee entitles you to advertise your property an unlimited number of times during the year through whichever system that particular university uses to inform students about properties to let. An added advantage is that most universities also allow their staff to view these databases, so you are targeting a large local employer for no extra cost.

As part of the registration process you will almost inevitably be asked to supply a copy of a landlord's gas safety certificate and electrical safety certificate. If your property is licensable you will also need to provide a copy of the licence issued to you by the council. You may also have to sign up to a code of standards or local accreditation scheme. Even if you do not have to pay a registration fee you may have to comply with other requirements. In Brighton and Hove, for example, both universities allow landlords to register free of charge, but require them to cap their rents on any properties advertised.

Advertising

Once you have jumped all these particular hurdles you will be registered on the university system and able to advertise. Most universities now have on-line database systems for advertising your property. These work well, as you can usually send in digital photographs of your property, which will help in attracting students. You may also be able to update property details yourself on line, so you can ensure that information is current, rather than relying on a probably overworked accommodation officer to do it for you.

In busy cities, university on-line databases are often password protected, so that only the students/staff at that particular institution are able to view the properties registered there. In some cities, however, the universities and FE institutions may co-operate more closely and share information with each other. Find out what happens in your target area as otherwise you may be missing out on a large pool of students at another local institution.

Case Study

Ms B, a classic case of bad timing

Ms B had contacted her existing group of postgraduate students in March to ask if they wanted to extend for the following year. Not receiving an answer from them, she advertised her property with the local university and started conducting viewings. Her current tenants then said they did want to stay on, but two of them were moving out and they were looking for two more. Ms B amended her listing to say that there were two vacant rooms and to contact the current occupants of the property to view.

By June there was still no sign of replacement tenants. As the tenancy did not end until mid-August Ms B was not too concerned, and she decided not to sign up the current tenants until there was a group of four. By the end of the tenancy, however, there was still no sign of two more tenants. As two of the existing group had left Ms B was now beginning to be out of pocket. To add to that, most current students had already found somewhere to live, meaning that those who were left were disorganised returning students or new first years. The remaining two tenants seemed to have no sense of urgency.

At that point she informed the current tenants that she wished them to sign a tenancy agreement by mid-September, for the whole property, whether or not they had found two new tenants. Fortunately this galvanised them into action and the house was full by the end of September. However, Ms B had lost the equivalent of three weeks' full rent and, as she had allowed the current tenants to stay on without giving them notice and had not bound them to a new tenancy for the full property, she was lucky to get off so lightly. ■

HOUSE-HUNTING DAYS
Some universities will organise special 'house-hunting' days, usually during the summer vacation, for new and returning students, where there will be some sort of social event, possibly a night in a hall of residence, housing advice talks, and then a list of

available accommodation given to each group. The purpose of this is to help students get together with other like-minded people and make sure they are fully informed about renting locally before they are let loose on innocent and unsuspecting landlords. If you are well known and favoured by the accommodation office, you may even be invited along yourself to meet possible tenants, perhaps even to give a talk on the landlord perspective (it happens!). These days are particularly useful if you have left it until the summer vacation before advertising your property.

Each day will usually be tailored to a specific type of student, e.g. postgraduates, mature students, international students, etc. If you are hoping to let your property on one of these days it goes without saying that you or someone you trust must be available all day to show groups round, give information about the property and be geared up to take deposits, sign tenancies, etc.

HEAD LEASING SCHEMES

Head leasing is a process by which you, the property owner, let your property direct to an institution, such as a university and they then sub-let the property on to the occupants, e.g. students. The advantages for you are that you are guaranteed the rent (usually paid termly in advance) by a stable, financially responsible organisation, whether or not the property is occupied. The institution will also take over the responsibility for finding tenants, drawing up agreements, dealing with any voids and rent arrears, inspecting and usually arranging for minor repairs to be carried out (with your permission and for which you would be billed). The institution is responsible for ensuring that your property is returned to you in good order and often they ensure it is professionally cleaned at the end of the tenancy.

Although head leasing offers similar benefits (particularly if you do not live near by) it is a different legal arrangement from having a managing agent as the institution becomes the landlord to the occupiers, whereas a managing agent merely acts as your agent. The main disadvantage with most head leasing schemes is that they will not usually take on your property for a full 52-week year. Some universities offer lets of as little as 41 weeks, others will go up to 48 weeks.

It is possible that head leasing schemes will become less popular with universities in the future as many are not profitable and are labour intensive. There are signs that some institutions are turning to property management instead, along the lines of commercial managing agents.

LETTING/MANAGING AGENTS

I would always recommend using a university accommodation office to advertise your property, rather than a letting agent – but then I am biased. Although most students will try their own university accommodation office first, going to letting agents follows shortly afterwards if they can't find what they want. So letting agents can be useful, particularly if you are not confident in your ability to be firm about tenancies, standing orders and guarantors. They are also useful for conducting viewings if you do not want or are not able to do these yourself. Of course, they will charge for their service – usually the equivalent of one month's rent, which can be a high price to pay for something you should be able to do yourself.

Please note that in this chapter I am referring to the service agents provide in terms of letting your property, rather than managing it. In Chapter 8 I will talk about agents in terms of managing your property, which is a separate service most letting agents offer.

If you are going to use a letting agent make sure they know when to advertise your property. In some towns and cities letting agents will work closely with local universities to ensure they are marketing properties at the same time that students are looking. They may even be registered with the university and able to use their on-line systems. In other towns/cities relations between universities and letting agents are slightly more strained and agents may not be timing the marketing of your property as well as they could. Some agents are a bit behind the game and think it's OK to advertise a property a month before the student wants to move in. It can be OK, but it's a risky strategy with students, as mentioned earlier.

When selecting a suitable letting agent it is worthwhile speaking to the university accommodation officers to get an unbiased view of who does a good job. Most universities will provide a list of letting agents who let to students. If an agent is not on that list, don't use them – they either treat students badly or they are not well known for letting to students (in which case it's pointless using them).

ON-LINE DATABASES

If you are not yet computer literate it is still possible for you to let your property, but it will be harder to compete with other landlords more willing to embrace new technology. Most students are computer savvy these days and expect the information they need to be available on line. Even if the university you are dealing with does not offer an on-line database to registered landlords, you can still make use of a number of other available sites. Some of these are free of charge, others will charge an advertising fee. All of them will offer the opportunity for you to upload photos of your property and the ability to manage the information you provide on-line. A couple of popular on-line sites are listed below – try searching on Google for others local to where you have your property.

www.accommodationforstudents.com
www.studentpad.co.uk

Plan B

For those of you who have tried every other method to no avail, or if you've got a nasty void period in the middle of the academic year, there are other ways of reaching potential tenants.

◆ University noticeboards – either in the accommodation office or in the Student Union.

◆ Noticeboards in popular student cafes/bars, meeting places, etc (although you may need a bit of insider information as to where such places are – not likely to be anywhere you would frequent on a regular basis unless you are a particularly 'hip' landlord!).

◆ Local newspapers/publications – they will usually have a particular day of the week which is known for property articles, ads, etc.

◆ Local language schools – usually run shorter courses, but often looking for properties for their over 18 year old students.

♦ Local hospitals – may want details of properties suitable to let to student nurses.

♦ Holiday lets – if you are in a tourist area of course. It's worth a try, particularly if you only need to let for a couple of months before the next academic year starts. Be prepared to provide a lot more equipment than you would normally have to.

SUMMARY

♦ Register with your local university accommodation office(s).

♦ Find out when it is best to advertise to different types of students.

♦ Decide when you are going to advertise and if you are going to use an agent.

♦ Sort out a Plan B.

Selecting Tenants

IN THIS CHAPTER

Organising viewings

Application form

Under 18s

References

Deposits

Guarantors

Signing up

If you have followed the details of the previous chapter you are now in the position of knowing when your property is to be advertised and what the likely volume of response is to be. You now need to maximise the chances of selecting a nice, well-organised group of students who will treat your property with respect and pay their rent on time. If you are using a letting agent to select your tenants you do not need to read this chapter (other than to understand the process).

ORGANISING VIEWINGS

If your property is to be advertised at the peak time of year, i.e. when the university has its first 'listing' date, you are likely to be inundated with phone calls and emails for the first few days. Of course, this maximises your chances of getting a good group of students, but it does mean that you have to be well organised to make the most of it.

The first thing you need to do is decide when you are going to be available for conducting viewings. You also need to ensure that your current tenants are not pestered for days on end by groups of students looking at the property. I would recommend that you select one day only for viewings in consultation with your tenants. As you will be aware from Chapter 4, you need to have permission from your tenants to enter the property and so you need their co-operation for this stage of the process. Confirm the viewing date with them and ask them to tidy up as much as possible the day before. To get maximum effort, you could offer to pay them!

If you are not able to conduct viewings yourself you could also offer to pay your tenants to show the property for you. However, this does have disadvantages – you will not be meeting your prospective tenants and your current tenants have the opportunity to list any problems and complaints they have with the property!

If you have several properties, select a different viewing day for each property and then you can meet all your prospective tenants (although this becomes impractical if you have a large number of properties).

Coping with enquiries

Assuming you are advertising at the peak time, have selected a viewing day, have forewarned your tenants and have cleared your diary for the day, you are now ready to receive enquiries from keen applicants. I recommend the following process.

◆ Answer any initial enquiries about the property.

◆ Inform applicants about the viewing date and book a time slot with them (allow half an hour) – state that all members of the group have to view at the same time.

◆ Take a contact name, telephone number and email address from one of the group.

◆ Confirm the booking by email and send them an application form (see below) for them to complete and give to you at the viewing, a draft tenancy agreement for them to read through, clear directions on how to get to the property and who to contact if they wish to cancel the viewing.

◆ Inform them you will be asking to see their student ID at the viewing.

- When you have filled up all your available viewing slots, take contact details of any further interested groups and keep them on a waiting list in case you get any cancellations.

Viewing day

On the day of the actual viewings get to the property half an hour before the first booking to ensure that your tenants have tidied up and the property is looking its best (within reason). During each visit show the group every room in the property and any outside space, explain what your application process is and answer any other questions they may have. Collect their completed application form from them at this stage (cross-checking with their student ID) and let them know that, if they are interested in proceeding, you will take up references.

If, as often happens, not all of the group turn up to the viewing, explain that you will prioritise offering the property to a group where all the tenants have viewed. The reasons for this are these.

- A complete group have organised themselves properly and are likely to organise everything else efficiently.

- All members of the group have seen the property and are aware of what they will be signing up for and who is going to have which room.

- You have met everyone and have an idea of how stable the group is.

APPLICATION FORM

I recommend that you issue application forms to students interested in your properties. This way you have a record of their main details in a format you can easily see and store. As well as their names and addresses, make sure you get the name of their educational institution and registration or student number, so that you can check with the institution that they are who they say they are.

It is also important that you get their parental home address. This is in case they ever do a moonlight flit and you need to pursue them through the courts for unpaid rent. If you are asking for a rental guarantor you will get this information anyway as part of that process. Mature students and some other students may not be able to provide you with a parental home address.

An example application form is shown in Appendix 2.

UNDER 18s

It is not very likely that you will find an under 18 year old in your group of tenants, but it is possible. Legally this can cause a bit of a problem. Although minors can enter into contracts for necessities (which includes accommodation) they cannot hold a legal estate, such as a tenancy. Effectively this means that you would be giving them a licence to occupy, rather than a tenancy.

Another problem is that the courts will not let you enforce a contract against a minor. The best way of dealing with this is to ensure that you have their parents acting as guarantors (see more below) so that, if necessary, you can enforce the contract against them.

REFERENCES

Despite what everyone else says, references are not as useful as one might think. However, it is still the norm to ask for them and you may as well do so. The problem with references is that if a student thinks he or she is unlikely to get a good reference from a previous landlord they will probably make one up. I have no evidence for this, but I do know that, as a university, there are a number of students leaving our residences each year who we would not be prepared to give a reference for. Oddly enough, we are never asked for references for those particular students. I can only assume that either their private sector landlord has not asked them for reference details, or the students concerned have provided a false one (or come up with some other reason as to why they cannot provide a reference).

If you have an applicant who states that they cannot provide a university reference because they have not lived in halls of residence, double check with the university. The university may not give you the information on data protection grounds, but if you do find out the student lived in halls of residence, but does not seem to want to give the university as a referee, be suspicious. On the other hand, students are often very silly in their first year away from home and may get themselves into situations which they subsequently would not repeat when they go out into the private rented sector (not least because they suspect a private rented landlord will have less patience than a university landlord!).

Making sure you get the rent

Now that students have to pay fees for their education it is probably worth while checking with a university that your group are not in debt with the university, even if they have never lived in halls. If a student is behind with their fee payments, they are more likely to fall behind with their rent. You will need to get permission from the group to ask for this information though.

Even if you do get a dubious reference or no reference at all for a student, use your commonsense before rejecting your student group (particularly if you don't have a queue of waiting groups for your property). If a student has got into problems paying rent before, you could ask them to pay all the rent in advance as a condition of granting the tenancy. If a student has caused damage in a previous property, you could double the deposit you take instead (but not to more than the equivalent of two months' rent – see section on deposits below). Of course, there is an element of risk with these suggestions – there are a few very bad student tenants out there and, in the end, you will probably use your gut instinct as much as any information you get from references.

A suggested reference request letter is illustrated in Appendix 3.

If the student has provided details of another private sector landlord as their referee I believe you get a far better picture of the student if you ring the landlord and ask the questions, rather than rely on a written response. People are much more likely to give you a fuller picture on the phone than they are in writing.

If you are not happy with the references you get back for your student group, you are at liberty to turn them down. You do not have to give them the specific reasons although it would be helpful to them if they knew which one of the group was not suitable.

DEPOSITS

Deposits (or bonds) are a payment made by the tenants, and held by the landlord (or an independent third party) to cover any specified breaches of the tenancy agreement by the tenant. The

tenancy agreement must specify the amount of the deposit and
what it is being held for. Most deposits will be used to cover any
damages occurring during the tenancy and any rent outstanding
at the end of the tenancy. Legally the deposit money belongs to
the tenant unless the landlord has a valid claim against it, so
should be returned within a reasonable time after the end of the
tenancy.

Tenancy Deposit Protection Schemes

From 6 April 2007, all deposits taken as part of assured
shorthold tenancies in England and Wales have to be registered
with a statutory tenancy deposit scheme. There are two types
of scheme: a free custodial scheme (where deposits are paid into
a separate account managed by the scheme) and insurance-
based schemes where the landlord or agent will hold the
deposit and any failure on his/her part to repay it to the tenant
will be covered by the scheme's insurance arrangements. The
insurance-based schemes will be funded through a fee paid by
landlords or agents. Both types of scheme will be free to the
tenants and, with the custodial scheme, the tenant even gets
some interest back from the deposit being held. Most landlord
associations and letting agents will be a member of one of the
insurance-based schemes and landlord associations will
probably offer a discount on the fee if you are one of their
members.

It is worth noting that the scheme only applies to assured
shorthold tenancies. This means that, if you are letting out a
flat in a building in which you live, or are letting out rooms in
your own home, you cannot offer an assured shorthold tenancy

---

and, therefore, do not have to lodge a deposit with one of the schemes. Another exception is any tenancy which has an annual rent of over £25,000 per annum – such tenancies are not assured shorthold tenancies. Any house let to a group of five students at over £85 a week each for a twelve-month period will, therefore, be exempt from the scheme. This will apply to many tenancies in London and the South East.

Any dispute at the end of the tenancy will be resolved by an alternative dispute resolution service which will be free to both parties. For up-to-date information on the schemes, see the DCLG website: *www.communities.gov.uk/tenancydeposit*

You should ensure that the deposit is taken at the time that the tenancy is signed. Usually the deposit will be equivalent to one month's rent, but it can be more or less than this. It should not equate to more than two months' rent, however, as it can then be classed as a premium, which means that the tenant can pass the tenancy on to another party (assign the tenancy) without your agreement. As good practice you should hold tenancy deposits in a separate account from your own money or other money related to your letting business.

A holding deposit

In the period of time between a group of students agreeing to take a property and them actually signing the tenancy, some landlords take a **holding deposit**. This is a payment made by the tenants to demonstrate their good faith and acknowledging the fact that you are holding the property specifically for them for a designated period. If you do decide to take such a deposit make sure you give the tenants a receipt which states how much they have paid, what the payment is for and in what circumstances the payment will be refunded. If you then go ahead with the tenancy the holding deposit should be deducted from the deposit payable upon signing the agreement.

If you impose a non-refundable holding deposit you are actually requesting a **premium**. Although this is legal most students are advised not to pay such charges and would think twice about taking on such a property, particularly if the sum is substantial.

Retainers

There is some confusion between holding deposits and **retainers**. It is a grey area, but most students and their advisors would view a retainer as an amount of money paid to cover a period when the property is empty and before the tenancy starts. In many university towns it is normal for student properties to be empty over the summer vacation. A retainer would normally be half rent paid for, say, two months, which acknowledges the fact that the tenants are not living in the property but will be starting their tenancy at a later date.

Usually the tenants would be able to use the property to store possessions. Retainers are not frequent in towns where there is a high demand for student properties as, in order to keep a popular property, students will be willing to pay full rent for a whole calendar year.

Settling disputes

Unfortunately disputes about deposits at the end of the tenancy are one of the most frequent complaints from tenants. As a result of this the government has introduced new legislation that applies to all assured shorthold tenancies, where a deposit is taken after 6 April 2007 (see box on page 78). In summary, it is a move greatly welcomed by tenants and viewed with apprehension by many landlords as they see yet more form-filling ahead.

GUARANTORS

It is becoming increasingly common for landlords to ask for parents of student tenants to act as rental guarantors for their offspring. Unfortunately, where a student is a member of a joint tenancy, the parent can unwittingly become a guarantor for every other member of the tenancy as well, because of their offspring's joint and several liability. It has been said that a guarantor is 'a fool with a pen' and many university accommodation offices are against the practice because of the problem of parents becoming liable for debts other than those of their own offspring.

From a landlord's perspective it is only sensible that a financially impecunious tenant has the back up of someone who is able to pay up if things go wrong. However, with the growing number of overseas students also looking for accommodation in the private sector, you may not always find it easy to obtain a UK guarantor for your tenants. It is common practice amongst letting agents to ask overseas students to pay the full amount of rent for the tenancy period in advance, in lieu of an acceptable guarantor.

If you decide you will ask for UK guarantors for your tenants, I would recommend that you word your guarantor agreement in such a way that it does not bind a particular parent to guarantee the debts of all members of the tenancy. You can use a phrase such as:

the Guarantor hereby guarantees to the Landlord to pay the rent reserved in the tenancy agreement up to a maximum of (total amount of rent divided by the number of tenants).

If you publicise this concession to your applicants, it will make your property more attractive to them and their parents and you will be seen as a landlord prepared to treat your tenants fairly.

SIGNING UP

You have finally agreed with a group of students that they will be renting your property. You now need to set aside a date to complete the paperwork so that the tenancy becomes binding on them. Don't hang around, if there are still a lot of other properties available they may change their minds and sign up with someone else. In advance of the signing day email all tenants a copy of the parental guarantor forms to be completed by their parents (if you are using them), standing order requests for them to complete, sign and bring with them and remind them to bring their cheque books or cash for the deposit (and first month's rent if you are asking them to pay that when they sign up).

You will already have given them a copy of the draft tenancy at the application stage, so they should be well aware by now of what they are letting themselves in for. Student Unions always advise students to get their tenancy agreements checked before signing, so yours should have had plenty of time to do this already.

On signing day ensure you have two printed copies of the tenancy agreement completed with the tenant names, the rent required, and the start and end dates of the tenancy period. In an ideal world the process should be as follows.

- Pass both copies of the tenancy agreement to all members of the group to sign each copy.

- Ask for cheques (or cash) for the deposit (and the first month's rent if you are collecting this now).

- Collect from each tenant a copy of your standing order instructions already completed with their bank details.

- Collect their parental guarantor forms (if applicable).

- Sign both copies of the tenancy agreement yourself and date them, then return one copy to the group.

Both parties are now bound by the agreement.

If, for some reason, not all your tenants can be physically present for signing, the above process can take place by post. Obviously this will take longer but, so long as you ensure that all the processes are complete before you sign and date the tenancy agreements, it will work just as well.

SUMMARY

- Set aside a viewing date or dates, in liaison with your existing tenants, and publicise this to enquirers.

- Be present at viewings if possible.

- Ensure interested parties have as much information as possible at an early stage and have a written application form completed by each person.

- Decide whether you are going to ask for guarantors.

- Take up references for all prospective tenants.

- Ask for standing order instructions in advance of signing the tenancy.

- Take deposits and store them securely and in accordance with legislation.

- Ensure you are the last person to sign the tenancy agreement so you can control when it becomes binding.

Moving In

IN THIS CHAPTER

Void inspection and annual maintenance

Cleaning

Inventories

House pack

Keys

Utility companies and council tax

Check-in

So you have selected your next tenants, have their deposits and possibly first month's rent as well. Your current tenants have moved out and you have dealt with any issues from that tenancy (see Chapter 9). Ideally, the property is empty for a short period between tenancies so you can get it in perfect condition for the next tenants.

VOID INSPECTION AND ANNUAL MAINTENANCE

You will already have done an inspection of the property before the last tenants moved out, so you should be aware of any major issues that need dealing with. However, there is no substitute for going through a property when it is empty and so much more is obvious once the posters, cushions and trailing electrical wires have left with the last occupants. There is a guideline inspection check sheet in Appendix 4 which you may find useful to use.

Go through the property, ticking off areas as you do them and noting anything that needs repair. There will be some jobs that need to be done annually which are ideally scheduled for the void time between tenancies. These include:

- gas safety certificate renewal
- servicing the vacuum cleaner
- cleaning carpets
- re-grouting around showers and baths
- cleaning and treating any condensation mould
- clearing out gutters
- cleaning external windows
- cutting back shrubbery in the garden (if there is one)
- sweeping chimneys (if applicable).

In addition, if you have agreed with the incoming tenants to do anything specific to the property (such as decorating the living area or replacing the sofa), make sure it is done before they move in. Even if you have not made an agreement with them in writing, you have made a verbal agreement and letting them down in this respect will get the whole landlord/tenant relationship off to a bad start.

Case Study

Mr G and the false promises

Five tenants agreed to take on a student house on the condition that the faulty shower was repaired or replaced and that the condensation mould in the bathroom was removed and the room redecorated. The landlord agreed verbally that the work would be done during the summer void period and the tenancies were then signed.

When the students moved in three months later they found that not only had the jobs agreed not been done, but that the washing machine door wouldn't open, the toilet seat was broken, bookcases and tables were broken, the oven was dirty, the vacuum cleaner not working, there was no hot water in the bathroom and the plug for the kettle administered electric shocks. When these matters were brought to the landlord's attention he dealt with most of them within three to four weeks. However, the agreed work to the bathroom and shower was never carried out and, five weeks after moving in, the tenants awoke at 3am when a large portion of the ceiling in the upper landing came crashing down.

The tenants then contacted the university accommodation office as well as local environmental health officers. One tenant moved out and never returned. The EHOs wrote to the landlord asking him to remedy the list of complaints within three weeks and the university accommodation office, having noted that this complaint was the latest of several about this landlord over the last few years, removed him from their register. As both local universities liaised over problem landlords, the other institution also removed him from their register. ■

CLEANING

You will probably have to do some cleaning between tenancies. Ideally the last tenants will have cleaned adequately to get their deposit back, but it is unlikely that they will do a proper 'deep' clean that a property needs every now and then, particularly one which has the high wear and tear of several young adults living in it.

There is a wide variation between landlords as to the standard they expect a property to be cleaned to at the end of a tenancy. If you do expect the tenants to leave the property in a condition which is of a professional cleaning standard then you do need to say so in the tenancy agreement. You also need to ensure that the property is at that level of cleanliness when they move in. So if your last tenants have not left the property professionally clean, then you must employ a professional cleaning company to clean it for you and deduct the charge from their deposit. The same goes for carpets – if you want the tenants to pay for them to be professionally steam cleaned at the end of the tenancy, you must say so in the tenancy agreement and ensure that each new set of tenants moves into a property where the carpets are freshly steam cleaned.

Personally, I just expect tenants to leave the property in a 'clean enough' state. That is, they have dusted and vacuum-cleaned throughout, wiped clean the bathroom and kitchen and cleaned out the oven and fridge-freezer as well as cupboards and have also removed all their belongings. I fully expect to have to do some deeper cleaning myself between tenancies.

It is worth noting that, if you are doing some work to the property between tenancies, there is no point cleaning until the work is complete. In my experience builders never clean up after themselves adequately, even if they are supposed to in the contract.

INVENTORIES

Now that the property is in good repair and clean, you need to update your inventory. An inventory (or schedule of condition) is a list of all the items you are providing as part of the property and should also include the condition of those items as well as the condition of the décor of each room. It is *vital* that you provide an inventory and get it signed by the tenants shortly after they move in. It is a record of what you have provided them with and will serve as evidence if there is any dispute over the deposit at the end of the tenancy. An example inventory is provided in Appendix 1.

When you are compiling/updating your inventory, go through the property carefully noting any changes from last year. For example, a room which was described as 'freshly decorated' last year may now be 'good décor, two marks on wall l/h side of window'.

There are professional inventory services, many of which will also provide a digital record of your property on a cd. These services are quite expensive, however. You may find it worthwhile to take photographs of every room in the property, as well as any items particularly prone to dispute (e.g. the cleanliness of ovens) so that you have some pictorial evidence of the condition of the property to go with the inventory.

HOUSE PACK

It is useful for your tenants to have a central file where they have copies of any manuals for equipment in the property, a place to store their copy of the tenancy agreement and inventory as well as other useful information about the property and the local area. I normally use an A4 lever arch file with plastic pockets for the contents. Tenants normally seem to store these files in the kitchen, which means they get dirty pretty quickly!

Suggested contents of the house pack:

◆ Copy tenancy agreement.

◆ Inventory.

◆ Gas safety certificate (tenants' copy).

◆ Copy electrical safety certificate.

◆ Copy HMO licence (if applicable).

◆ Fire safety information.

- Copies of manuals for equipment provided.

- Notes about any peculiarities of the property, such as 'the drain at the side of the house quickly gets covered with street litter, ensure it is regularly cleared'.

- Emergency contact numbers for gas or water leaks or electricity failure, as well as your emergency contact number.

- Location of the water stop cock, and the gas and electricity meters.

- Information about refuse collection days and local recycling facilities.

- Bus/train timetables for university routes.

- Any useful local information such as nearest launderette, post office, banks, takeaways, etc.

- Anything else useful you can think of – some landlords I know even provide a manual on how to clean a house properly!

It's always a nice touch if you can provide something that welcomes your new tenants to the property, such as a bottle of wine in the fridge. I admit I have never done this, but I admire those who do!

KEYS

You will need to ensure that you have one set of keys for each tenant, plus a spare set (maybe two spare sets) for yourself. A set of keys should include whatever keys are used for the front door and a bedroom key (if you have individual locks on the bedrooms). You will also need to ensure that there is a key for the back door in the property and one key for any other lockable areas, such as sheds, garages or cellars. Make sure you have a copy of all the keys you provide.

It is worth noting that you do not automatically have a legal right to hold keys as the tenants have 'exclusive possession' of the property and can exclude you. However, in practice, most tenants would be horrified if they lost their keys and then couldn't get a copy from your set. It would mean paying for the locks to be changed, which would be far more expensive for them. So, unless you are misusing your keys by letting yourself into the property without notice, tenants will be perfectly happy for you to keep keys.

You will occasionally need to issue keys to contractors to carry out work during the tenancy. Remember that you need the tenants' permission to gain entry to the property unless it is an emergency. You should ensure that any contractors you use respect the tenants' rights and do not let themselves into the property at any time they choose without warning. (Female tenants, in particular, are horrified if they come out of the shower wearing nothing but a towel, to find a burly plumber leering at them while waiting to change a tap washer.)

If you have several properties it is worth keeping a key book where you record details and signatures of who keys are issued to.

UTILITY COMPANIES AND COUNCIL TAX

You will need to let various people know who is taking over the tenancy. All you need to do is telephone the gas, electricity and water companies with the names of your new tenants and the date they are moving in. They will ask you to provide them with a meter reading when the tenants take over the property. You will then get the bill for anything you have used while the property has been empty.

If the property is unfurnished, no water rates are due while the property is empty.

You may be aware that full time students are not liable for council tax. However, unless the local council is aware that students are living in your property they will continue to levy the full amount of council tax. In the absence of anyone else taking responsibility, the council will pursue you for any unpaid charges. It is, therefore, worth informing the council of the names of your tenants and which institution they are attending. The council will normally have an arrangement with the local educational institutions whereby they can check on which people are students. Make sure you keep copy tenancy agreements for six years, though, just in case the council try to pursue you in the future for some reason.

If you let your property to a mixed group of students and workers, then the workers in the group will be liable for the council tax. If there is only one worker they will get a 25% discount.

CHECK-IN

Make sure you have agreed a time to meet with your prospective tenants to hand over the keys. Let them know that they will need to allow at least half an hour for you to go through the property and inventory with them.

At the check-in you will need to do the following.

- Give them a copy of the inventory and explain that they will need to check and sign it within seven days.

- Walk through each room with the tenants pointing out anything they need to know and showing them how things like the shower, oven and boiler work.

- Show them what is in the house pack.

- Show them the location of the gas and electricity meters and take the readings – note the readings on both copies of the inventory.

- Show them where the bins and recycling boxes are and tell them which day is collection day.

- Point them in the direction of the nearest shops and bus stop or train station (hopefully they will already know this information).

- Hand over the keys!

SUMMARY

Before your tenants move in check the following:

- Repairs and required annual tasks are completed.

- The property is clean.

- The inventory is up to date and you have two copies.

- The house pack is updated.

- You have sufficient copies of all keys.

- You have informed utility companies and the council about your new tenants.

- You have confirmed a check-in time with the tenants.

- Complete the check-in process as above and leave them to it.

Managing the Let

IN THIS CHAPTER

Managing agents

Inspections

Maintaining your property during the tenancy

Rent payments and managing arrears

Harassment and illegal eviction

Noise and neighbour disputes

Voids and changes

Extending the tenancy

Managing parents

It should go without saying that your student property is a significant investment of your time and money and it is prudent to ensure that the occupants you have selected are treating your investment with due respect or, in legal terms, in a 'tenant-like manner'. It is also the case that dealing with property or tenant problems at an early stage will prevent greater loss of time and revenue later on. Whether you employ a managing agent to see to this area or deal with it yourself (to be recommended wherever possible) this chapter will provide advice on the day-to-day running of the let.

MANAGING AGENTS

Ideally you will be residing close enough to your investment to ensure that you can manage it effectively, i.e. to be able to visit the property at relatively short notice. However, in some circumstances this will not be possible and you will need to engage the services of a managing agent. As with selecting your tenant, selecting your managing agent should be a careful process. If you have already used an agent to let your property then you will probably already be aware of the levels of property management that they can provide. Most letting agents will also offer a management service – usually at two different levels.

◆ A basic level will be to deal with requests from the tenant for repairs to be dealt with and to ensure that safety certificates are updated when necessary.

◆ A higher level of service (at a higher fee) will also collect your rent for you and provide a rental guarantee.

Most university towns will have a large selection of letting/ managing agents. The first thing is to ensure that your prospective agent is not frowned upon by the university. While agents are very good at selling themselves to potential customers, they can forget that the clients who are in the most contact with them are the student occupants themselves. Students are very quick to complain to their university housing office or student union if they believe their home is not being looked after properly by the agent. Whereas the level of expectation as to the service which should be provided increases annually, accommodation offices and student unions will take note if a particular agent's name crops up regularly and if complaints are not dealt with promptly.

As a tardy response to requests for repairs can adversely affect your property, you would do well to note any signs that a managing agent is not up to scratch in the eyes of the accommodation department.

Case Study

Working with the universities

In one university town one managing agent had a particularly bad reputation with both universities, based on some serious complaints from students in the past. Even though this agency was now under new management it was still not listed on the lists of agencies provided to students by both institutions. However, because it charged lower fees than average to landlords, it was still popular with landlords and managed a large number of properties although many students only used it if they could find nothing else suitable.

The new manager of the agency was concerned at the lack of support from the universities and made appointments to speak to the accommodation managers at both institutions and outlined the changes that had been made at the agency. He also undertook to personally deal with any complaints that came from either university. As a result of this the agency was once again listed with both universities and experienced a corresponding rise in enquiries from students. True to his word the manager regularly liases with the university and no complaints from students have been received in the past two years. ■

You will, of course, be comparing agencies in terms of the management fee that they charge. This is important, but a lower fee and bad service will affect you in a more long-term adverse way than a higher fee and good service. If you can, find out about the agencies in your area from other landlords. Joining a local landlords' association will help you to meet others in your situation and you may pick up some useful tips as to which agents to use.

Choosing an agent

My personal view is that, if you have no other way of knowing which agent to use, picking one that is new to the scene and therefore keen to make a good impression and build up a good reputation is better than going for the biggest in the market. The bigger agencies may be useful if you are using them to find students (as outlined in Chapter 5), but if you have found your own students and just need someone to manage the property for you then size really doesn't matter. Those agencies who have been around for longer and are bigger are often complacent about their standing and neglect the needs of their landlord customers as much as they do their student ones.

At the very least I recommend that you put the following list of questions to your prospective agent and note their answers.

♦ How often will you inspect the property?

♦ Will I get a report on the condition of my property after you have inspected it?

♦ What is your method for ensuring that gas and electrical safety certificates are kept up to date?

♦ What are your standard response times for different categories of repair?

♦ What is your performance overall in meeting those response times?

♦ How do you select who carries out repairs on managed properties?

♦ Are you a member of an organisation responsible for standards within the letting industry (such as ARLA)?

♦ If we have a dispute, is there an independent party who can resolve it?

Case Study_____

Ms E and the managing agent

Ms E lived in Brighton, but was moving away and wanted to let out her own home until she was ready to sell it. Knowing that I had some knowledge of local agents, she asked me to recommend one to manage her property for her as she did not feel she had the confidence to manage the let herself. I gave her the details of two local agents who I knew offered a good service to both tenants and landlords. However, she eventually selected a larger, cheaper agent on the grounds that 'he seemed to know what he was talking about'.

A few months later I noticed that a glass pane in the front door of her property was broken. When I telephoned her she said the tenant had made her aware of this and the agent was to replace it. Two months and several phone calls later it was eventually replaced. In the meantime she discovered that her gas safety certificate had elapsed without being renewed by the agent (a service which he was due to perform under their contract) thus leaving her criminally liable.

When she then attempted to end her management contract with the agent, he pointed to the clause in the agreement stating that she had to give three months' notice, despite her having ample cause to terminate the contract on poor customer service grounds. Eventually, unwilling to pursue the matter further, she moved to one of the agents I recommended but lost two months' fees as a result. ■

You will note that I have omitted any questions relating to the collection of rent. In my experience managing agents are extremely good at ensuring that rent is collected promptly from tenants. I also expect that you will remember to ask what the agent's charges are for managing your property!

INSPECTIONS

Assuming that you are managing your property yourself, I would always recommend that you inspect your property at regular intervals, for the following reasons.

♦ To ensure that any disrepair to the property, such as damp, is dealt with before it can cause serious damage to your investment.

♦ To ensure that any safety problems, such as loose paving stones, loose wires, etc, are dealt with before you find yourself with a damages claim under the Defective Premises Act 1972.

♦ To ensure that the occupants are treating the property in a 'tenant-like manner', i.e. not causing damage, maintaining those things they are responsible for, clearing away rubbish, etc.

♦ To ensure that there is no evidence of occupants other than those you contracted with staying there permanently (of course your tenants should be permitted to have guests) – this is particularly important if your property is three or more storeys and you have let it to four occupants. A fifth occupant will render you licensable as an HMO and all that entails (see Chapter 3).

♦ If you are operating a relevant HMO (i.e. letting to more than two unrelated people in the same property) you have a duty to ensure that the common areas of the property are kept in good repair.

Always ensure that you give your tenants at least 24 hours' notice (preferably in writing) before you visit. This is a legal requirement and also has the advantage that they are more likely to tidy up and thus make it easier for you to inspect. Although you will be just as interested in ensuring that your property is not falling down around their ears due to some maintenance problem, they will rightly assume that you will be checking up on them as well! I would advise you to inspect your property at least every six months, but not more than once every couple of months. Any more than this could be construed as verging on harassment.

Unless you have some relevant experience or qualifications in building construction or maintenance, you may find it useful to have a checklist of areas to inspect as you go along. I have, therefore, provided for your convenience a copy of the one used by the University of Sussex when inspecting its small off-campus properties (Appendix 4). Obviously any problems you discover should be dealt with as soon as possible.

Do not, under any circumstances, use the visit as an opportunity to criticise your tenants' mode of living, moral behaviour or conduct towards each other, unless it is something that materially affects your property. Do not be surprised, if your visit is before midday, to find half your tenants still in bed, often with a member of the opposite sex (or in Brighton, sometimes with the same sex). Although this may offend your own sense of morality it has nothing to do with your occupation as a landlord and should not be commented upon, unless you have reason to believe that the guest has, in fact, become an extra occupant.

Illegal drugs

I should mention here a few words about illegal drugs. Many, if not most, students dabble with drugs to a greater or lesser extent. Although widely accepted it is still criminal behaviour and you will, no doubt, have a clause within your tenancy agreement, which forbids any criminal behaviour. Despite the widespread use of marijuana it is still an illegal drug and not many landlords are aware that, if they knowingly permit its use, they are themselves in breach of the law. Having said that, your local constabulary will not normally be interested in personal use of a Class C drug within someone's home.

If you find evidence of drug use during your inspection my advice, in order to protect yourself, is to warn your tenants, in writing, that drug use on the premises is forbidden by the tenancy agreement and that if you see any future evidence of it you will be obliged to inform the police. If, during your inspection, you see more serious evidence, such as widespread cultivation of marijuana or a stash of foil-wrapped blocks of a strange smelling substance in the corner of a student's bedroom (it's happened!), you should inform the police immediately.

MAINTAINING YOUR PROPERTY DURING THE TENANCY

Under the Landlord and Tenant Act 1985, you have a legal duty to ensure that the following are kept in good repair:

- the structure and exterior of the dwelling;
- basins, sinks, baths and other sanitary facilities;
- installations for the provision of hot water and heating.

In practice, student tenants will expect you to keep everything in repair.

After completing your inspection you may have a list of minor maintenance items that need to be dealt with. At other times your tenants may also ring to ask for something to be fixed. Unless you are gifted at DIY, the most useful person you can know as a landlord is a 'handyman'.[3] Major maintenance jobs can be dealt with by getting quotes from recommended builders, but nothing can replace the ongoing support of someone reliable to do all those fiddly little jobs such as changing washers, repairing window latches, drawer runners and fixing minor leaks. Find and nurture one as soon as you can.

Other people you will need to nurture are a CORGI registered gas engineer (to deal with boiler/heating problems as well as your gas safety certificate) and an electrician qualified to Part P of the NICIEC electricity regulations (or equivalent). At the time of writing, electricians are like gold dust as nearly all electrical work carried out in domestic properties has to be certified to be legal and HMOs should have an electrical safety certificate, usually renewed every five years. Not all electricians are qualified to the relevant standard and the ones that are qualified are much in demand and charge accordingly. If you do not know anyone reliable to use, ask your local university to recommend someone. They will often have a list of local contractors they use for their own or head leased properties.

If you are sending someone round to carry out maintenance, ensure your tenants are expecting them. Again, you should always ensure they have at least 24 hours' notice and that, if you have given a key to your contractor, they do not let themselves in without permission.

---

3   I recognise the sexism of this term however, in my experience, such useful people usually are men!

Empty periods

Particularly over the Christmas vacation, you may find your tenants plan to go home for 2–3 weeks. Remind them to keep heating on low to stop pipes freezing and to secure the property safely before they leave.

RENT PAYMENTS AND MANAGING ARREARS

If you followed my advice in Chapter 6, rent should be coming direct into your bank account from each of your tenants on a set date each month, timed to be there by the time your mortgage payment goes out. In most cases there will be no more problems until it is time to set up your next batch of tenants. However, occasionally you may run into problems with rent arrears. In a worst case scenario this may develop into full-blown non-payment of rent forcing you to take action to evict your tenants with all the attendant problems that brings. So it is always best to deal with rent arrears problems at the earliest opportunity.

Below is a timetable of how to deal with rent arrears. The more faint-hearted among you may feel that treatment in the early stages is harsh, but I must warn you that court action is lengthy and unpredictable, so proceed firmly from the very beginning in order to avoid more serious problems in the future. If you have not done this before, I recommend you get a solicitor to deal with it for you from the Notice Seeking Possession stage (if it gets that far) until you know what you are doing (or ask for help from you local landlord association).

Timetable of arrears from first missed payment

1. At the first sign of a late payment, ring/email your tenants to let them know that the payment has not gone through and to ask why. In most cases there will be an innocent reason and a

request for immediate payment (either in cash or by immediate bank transfer) will be met. **1 week**

2. If payment is not with you within seven days, follow up with a letter to the tenants (written to them jointly if they are on a joint tenancy, even if it is only one of them that is late paying) and point out that, under the terms of the tenancy, you are entitled to charge for any reasonable costs associated with chasing up late payments. Ask them to pay within the next seven days. If you are using guarantors send a copy of the letter to each of them.

At this stage your tenants may admit that they have a problem making that month's payment. Advise them to seek financial advice from their Student Union and state that you still expect to receive the next payment on the due date, but you are willing to negotiate on how to collect the current arrears.

2 weeks

3. If they agree to pay the next month and come up with a plan for how to pay this month, no problem. However, confirm any agreement in writing and state that failure to comply will mean they are putting their right to remain in the property at risk. **3 weeks**

4. When the next monthly payment is due, check to see if that has been paid. If it is paid then you now only need to check your tenant meets the agreement on paying back the last month's arrears. If it is not paid you should now issue the tenants with a Section 8 Notice of Intention to Seek Possession. **At this stage it is important that you get some legal advice** (at least until you have some practice at doing this) as

serving notice is a vital part of gaining possession and any tiny mistake in your form will render the whole process useless when the judge throws it out.

The notice has to be in the correct form (it is available from stationers) and you need to state the grounds for seeking possession. You will be able to use Ground 8, which is a mandatory ground (i.e. if proved, the judge has to award you possession) but, just in case the tenants pay some money between now and a court hearing, you should also state Ground 10 (behind with the rent) and Ground 11 (persistently late paying rent), both of which are discretionary grounds (i.e. the judge does not have to award you possession). Send a copy of the notice to the guarantors and keep a copy for your files.

5. To serve the notice on the tenants I always recommend that this is done in person and that you have an independent witness with you. In court you will have to supply a sworn affidavit that notice has been served in order to gain possession and you will not be able to do this if you send the notice by post. You will have stated on the notice when it expires (normally two weeks for rent arrears). By now most tenants will have realised that you are serious about taking action and will come up with your rent payment somehow.

5 weeks

6. However, if you have served Notice, two weeks have elapsed and there is still no sign of the full rent payment, you can apply to the local county court for a possession order. The court staff will tell you which forms to use. You will need to complete them fully, attach your evidence (e.g. rent statements,

evidence of serving notice) and send back to the court with the fee (£150 at the time of writing). You can state on the application that you wish to claim costs.   **7 weeks**

7. The court will then send a copy of the claim to the tenants and issue you both with a date for the hearing (usually a month later). The tenants can defend the claim (e.g. prove they have paid or counterclaim that you are in breach of the tenancy in some way, such as not doing repairs).   **8 weeks**

8. On the date of the hearing turn up to the court in plenty of time, together with your solicitor, if you are using one. Or, if you are a member of a landlord association (recommended), they might be able to arrange for someone to attend with you until you know what you are doing.   **12 weeks**

9. Assuming that you have proof of substantial rent arrears, you will be granted possession within 14 days, or a suspended possession, which will require the tenants to pay the rent due plus a regular amount towards the arrears. If there is a suspended possession order and the tenants fail to meet the stated conditions you can reapply to the court for full possession.   **14–20 weeks**

10. The tenants should move out on the stated possession date. If they do not you are not allowed to re-enter the property yourself! You then (frustratingly) have to reapply to the court to enforce the order. This means paying another fee to arrange for bailiffs to enter the property and evict the occupants. You then get your property back at last and, having a judgment for arrears, are free to pursue the guarantor (if you have any) or the tenants themselves for the outstanding payment.

Again, this can be done through the courts by either sending bailiffs to collect goods (useful to have car registration numbers!), or by issuing an attachment of earnings order which requires an employer to pay you the money owed out of the debtor's salary.   **22–26 weeks**

Don't let this section put you off too much. Serious rent debt is relatively rare. Based on my own experience within a university, I would estimate that only about 3% of students get to the stage of having to be issued with a Notice, and less than 1% would eventually get as far as a court hearing.

Nevertheless, planning for the worst means that you and your tenants are clear on where the boundaries lie and serves as a reminder that your relationship is a business one, not a personal friendship.

HARASSMENT AND ILLEGAL EVICTION

It will have been clear from the section above that following a recognised legal procedure to evict a tenant is imperative. Just because you own a property does not give you the right to claim it back whenever you want. Even if you are sharing part of your own home you do have to give 'reasonable notice' if you want someone to leave (usually four weeks), although you do not have to get a court order.

Unlawfully depriving a tenant of any part of the premises is a criminal offence and can lead to compensation being awarded to a tenant. Changing the locks while tenants are away and refusing them access is illegal eviction.

Harassment is also a criminal offence and is defined as:

◆ doing acts likely to interfere with a residential occupier's peace or comfort; or

◆ persistently withdrawing or withholding services.

Unfortunately, many landlords find it difficult to 'let go' of a property and insist on 'popping round' frequently to check up on things – even letting themselves into the property if the tenants are not there. As a landlord you do not even have an automatic right to hold a spare key to the property (although for practicality's sake it is normal for most landlords to hold spare keys). If you misuse your key by letting yourself into the property the tenants are perfectly within their right to change the locks and refuse to give you a key, as they have the right to exclude you from the property as part of the tenancy. The only exceptions to this are specific visits notified to them in advance and for purposes stated in the tenancy agreement, such as inspection and repair.

Case Study

Mrs D – interfering mother

A group of students approached a university accommodation office to complain that the mother of their landlord was always letting herself into their house and even coming into their bedrooms unannounced. On one occasion she had accused a female student of being 'dirty and immoral' because she had a male guest in her room.

A meeting was held at the accommodation office between the students, the landlord and her mother. There was a heated and tearful exchange between the mother and the accused student, but it was finally agreed that the landlord would deal with the property herself from now on, and the mother was kept away from the business as she could not accept that her unannounced visits and moral opinions constituted harassment of the tenants. ■

NOISE AND NEIGHBOUR DISPUTES

A house full of student tenants can be noisy. If you are getting complaints from neighbours about your tenants speak to them informally first. They may be unaware of the impact of their actions on others. Student lifestyles are very different from working people and a student who staggers in from a nightclub at 3am, laughing with friends and slamming the front door, is going to cause a working neighbour a huge amount of irritation which will build up over the next few sleepless hours and erupt into angry phone calls to you and possibly threatened violence to the tenants.

Point out to your tenants that noise audible outside the premises late at night is in breach of their tenancy agreement and can constitute a nuisance. The local authority have a duty to investigate noise complaints, and can impose hefty fines and remove offending equipment such as stereos and speakers.

If your tenants continue to cause problems it is worth contacting their university to complain. There has been a lot in the press over the past couple of years about a process known as 'studentification' which is the takeover of areas of a town by a large influx of students and the negative effect that has on the existing population. Universities are sensitive about their local image and can seek to take action against students under their own contract with them if they are seen to be 'bringing the university into disrepute'.

Of course, you are also able to take action against your own tenants and, in some cases, may be required to enforce the tenancy and take steps to evict them if they persist in causing a nuisance to other residents.

VOIDS AND CHANGES

It is likely that, at some point, one member of a group of students is going to want to move out during the tenancy. Often this is because they are dropping out of their course and returning home, or sometimes it is because they have fallen out with the other tenants. If you are letting to a group of first year undergraduates it is even more likely that someone will drop out. Clearly, dropping out of the course does not give a tenant the right to waive their liability to you.

If one of your tenants approaches you mid-tenancy to say they want to move out, you will need to point out that they are still responsible for the rent. However, it is reasonable for you to say that their liability will end once a new tenant is found to replace the one leaving. They may already have someone in mind, in which case you will just need to vet them in the same way you would a new group.

Case Study
Does a landlord have a duty to mitigate his loss?

Until very recently, it had always been thought that if a tenant moved out mid-tenancy, they were liable for the rent for the remainder of the term but that the landlord had a duty to 'mitigate his loss' by making efforts to re-let the property. However a recent Court of Appeal decision (Reichmann and Dunn v Beveridge and Gauntlett, [2006] EWCA Civ 1659) held that a landlord is under no obligation to mitigate his loss when seeking to recover rent due under a lease where a tenant had abandoned the property. Although the case concerned a commercial lease the reasoning applies just as much to residential tenancies.

Notwithstanding this decision, it is probably always a good idea to try to re-let a void property, even if the tenants are still liable for the rent, because the practical effect otherwise is that you are likely to have to take court action to enforce your rights. ▪

If there is no one yet available to take over the room, the students themselves will be able to make use of on-line message boards at university and you should help them by re-advertising the room in the property via your normal methods.

When a new person is found there are two ways to handle the change in tenancy legally.

♦ Accept the leaving tenant's notice as ending the tenancy for all tenants and issue a new tenancy agreement to the remaining tenants and the new person.

♦ Or complete a 'transfer of tenancy' form (see Appendix 5) whereby the leaving tenant, the remaining tenants, the incoming tenant and yourself all sign a form to say that the leaving tenant's interest in the tenancy is agreed to pass to the incoming tenant. The incoming tenant should pay a deposit to the leaving tenant and this should be acknowledged in the form.

If you choose the first method you will need to check the leaving tenant's room and release their deposit (or make a claim against it) before the new tenant moves in. You may also need to update the inventory.

EXTENDING THE TENANCY

If you are fortunate enough to have a group of tenants who wish to stay on for the next academic year, you can handle this in one of two ways.

- Let the current fixed term expire and allow the tenancy to continue with both parties continuing as before. The tenancy then becomes a 'statutory periodic' tenancy and continues with all the same terms and conditions, except that if the tenants want to leave, they only need to give you one month's notice (or four weeks if they are paying rent weekly) and, if you want to end the tenancy, give the tenants two months' notice (or eight weeks, if they are paying rent weekly). Both notice periods would run from the next available rent day.

- If you want to change any details of the tenancy (normally you will be putting the rent up) you will need to issue a new tenancy agreement with the new details – and you will probably wish to do this as a new fixed term.

MANAGING PARENTS

One of the unexpected complications of letting to students is that, all too often, you find you are dealing not only with four or five students, but four or five sets of parents as well. Parents are far more involved in the lives of their young adult offspring than they were 20 or 30 years ago, often because they are financing the rental costs themselves. Usually, however, parents will normally only get involved if some problem has arisen and a simple pleasant conversation putting forward your perspective on the problem usually resolves things. If it's a repair that needs doing, give them an estimate of when the work will be complete and let them know what you are doing to minimise any inconvenience to the tenants.

Sometimes, though, things can get out of hand. If you find you are often being contacted by parents over minor issues, or are dealing with a parent who is becoming increasingly abusive, it's time to put your foot down. Remind such parents that your contract is with the tenants and that, from now on, you will deal only with the tenants. If the parents wish to get written permission from the tenants asking you to deal with their parents instead, then you will do so but will correspond in writing (which can include email) to one named representative only (if your tenants are on a joint tenancy). It is then up to that tenant or nominated parent to circulate your communications with the others as they see fit. In all your communications, remain polite, pleasant and professional. Even though it can be frustrating to have to deal with the unreasonable demands of some parents, staying professional will help ensure a better outcome.

SUMMARY

◆ If you are employing a management agent, select them carefully and monitor their performance.

◆ Inspect your property regularly (say, every three months) but not so often that you are in danger of harassing your tenants.

- Ensure you have a good team of gas and electrical engineers and general handymen behind you.

- Keep an accurate record of rent payments and deal with any problems early on – don't be afraid to take firm action when necessary.

- Deal with any noise complaints from neighbours and enlist the help of the universities when you need to.

- Ensure you do not bother your tenants more than necessary, even if you think you are just being friendly.

- Be reasonable in accepting new tenants when someone wants to leave.

- If your current tenants want to extend, decide how the agreement will continue.

- Be firm about how much communication you will have with parents.

Moving Out

IN THIS CHAPTER

Timing

Serving Notice

End of tenancy letter

Check-out and return of deposit

TIMING

When you are letting to students it is important that you time tenancies to coincide with the academic year. This means that tenancies should end at some point between the end of June and the middle of September at the latest. Students do not wish to move when they are struggling with coursework, essay deadlines and exams. As mentioned in Chapter 7, ideally you will allow a short break between the end of a tenancy and the beginning of the next to allow for maintenance work to be done to the property.

SERVING NOTICE

Many landlords do not bother with the legal requirement of serving notice to end a tenancy. I suspect this is because they do not realise that a tenancy carries on past the end of a fixed term until any notice period expires. Fortunately, many tenants also assume that the end date of a fixed term spells the end of a tenancy and they think they have to move out. **However, unless you serve a valid notice seeking possession of your property, your tenants do not have to move out.**

Hopefully, as set out in Chapter 5, you will have ascertained some months before the end of the fixed term whether or not your tenants want to stay on for another year. If they do not wish to stay, you should serve them with a Section 21 Notice Seeking Possession at least two months (if rent is paid monthly) or eight weeks (if rent is paid weekly) before the end of the fixed term. If you do not serve this Notice your tenants are entitled to stay on in the property until the expiry of any valid Notice you do serve them with. Clearly, this could cause problems for new tenants planning to move in.

If you do serve them with the correct Notice (see Appendix 6) and they still do not move out, I am afraid that you then have to apply to the county court for possession of the property. For this purpose you can use the 'accelerated possession procedure' which is a quicker process than trying to gain possession on the grounds of a breach of tenancy.

Fortunately, ending up with sitting tenants is not a problem common in letting to students. On the whole students want to move out at the end of the academic year as they will already have made other arrangements.

END OF TENANCY LETTER

About a month before the tenancy is due to end I recommend that you send a letter to your tenants reminding them of what needs to be done before they return the property to you. You will need to say what standard of cleanliness you expect the property to be left in and notify them of any particular jobs they need to do under the tenancy agreement to ensure that their deposit is returned. Remind them also to contact utility companies to inform them of their forwarding addresses for final bills and also the council tax office. Give them a check-list that is easy to follow, such as below.

◆ Contact gas, electricity, telephone, water and television/internet service providers and inform them of the date you are leaving and your forwarding address for final bills.

◆ Contact the local council tax office to inform them you are leaving and your forwarding address.

- Arrange for the Post Office to forward your mail for a period of at least three months.

- Clean the property, including dusting, vacuum cleaning, washing down paintwork, cleaning mirrors and the inside of windows and thoroughly cleaning the bathroom and kitchen areas.

- Clean the oven according to the instructions in the manual.

- Defrost the fridge-freezer and clean when defrosted. Leave the doors slightly ajar when you have finished.

- Arrange for carpets to be steam cleaned (if this is required by the tenancy agreement).

- Tidy the garden and outside area, removing any of your own belongings.

- Remove all your belongings from the property.

- Ensure that rubbish is bagged up securely and disposed of.

You should also ask your tenants to let you have all of their forwarding addresses so that you can return their deposit to them as soon as possible. Arrange with your tenants what time you will meet with them on the final day to do the check-out.

CHECK-OUT AND RETURN OF DEPOSIT

Turn up to the property at the agreed time to do the final check-out. You can go through the inventory room by room with the tenants present, but I find I get distracted and prefer to do it properly once they have gone. Either way, it is best if you do it as soon as possible and make notes of anything that is missing or damaged. Also note how clean the property is and whether any unwanted possessions have been left for you to dispose of. Check the meters, and take readings and check that all copies of the keys have been returned.

If there is any damage, or the property has not been left as clean as specified in the tenancy agreement, you are permitted to make deductions from the deposit. However, you must be as fair as possible. Deposit deductions are a source of great resentment with tenants and can end up taking up an awful lot of your time dealing with angry phone calls from ex-tenants and/or their parents. Now that this whole area is regulated by Tenancy Deposit Schemes, you will need to be even more careful.

Before you decide to deduct some money from the deposit, ask yourself these questions.

- Does the tenancy agreement allow me to deduct money for X?
- Did I make the tenants aware of the fact that I would expect X to be done?
- Can X be considered 'fair wear and tear' (see below)?
- Is X a small amount of money to put right (say, under £20)?

If you can answer 'yes' to the first two questions and 'no' to the second two, then go ahead and deduct. It is a good idea to take digital photographs of any damage or cleaning for which you are claiming.

Fair wear and tear
There is a lot of confusion and misunderstanding as to what

constitutes 'fair wear and tear'. Clearly, in being used, a property
and its contents deteriorate over time. One does not expect a
cooker to look as pristine as the day it was bought, or a table to
have the same sheen as it did when it was first installed in the
property. But does a chip on the melamine surface of a kitchen
table count as damage, or fair wear and tear? How about a
wooden chair, with a leg that has come unglued from the seat?

In the end, you have to use your judgment and ask yourself if it is
worth the hassle of claiming for something that might be argued
against vociferously by the tenants. Most tenants would expect to
be charged for something that is actually broken or no longer
useable, such as a cracked mirror. However, they would feel
unjustly treated if they were charged for something that might
have worked loose, such as a toilet seat or chair leg, or with
minor damage such as a dent in the wall where the door handle
has banged against it, or a small mark on a table. If you feel that
is unfair to you, as a landlord, it is worth remembering that every
year you can claim 10% of the rent you receive for depreciation of
furnishings and offset it against tax.

Next steps in making a deduction

If you do decide to make a deduction from the deposit, make sure
that you put your claim in writing and back it up with estimates
or invoices for work required. If you are claiming for the
replacement of items of furniture, you should allow for a certain
amount of depreciation depending on how long you have had the
piece being replaced. It is fair to assume that you would replace
something after ten years anyway, so if you are replacing an eight
year old sofa because the frame has been broken, you should only
charge 20% of the new replacement cost. Return any balance

from the deposit to the tenants at the same time as you send your claim.

If you are unfortunate enough to have claims amounting to more than the amount of deposit you are holding, you can take the ex-tenants to the small claims court for the balance if they refuse to reimburse you.

SUMMARY

◆ Ensure your tenancy ends at a time that is relevant for student lets.

◆ Serve a Section 21 Notice at least two months before the end of the fixed term.

◆ Send a letter with a check-list of tasks to be completed by the tenants before they return the property to you.

◆ Do a final check of the property at the end of the tenancy and take meter readings.

◆ Think carefully about whether it is worthwhile making any claims against the deposit.

◆ If you are making a deposit deduction inform the tenants as soon as you can, providing evidence and receipts where possible and returning any balance of the deposit due to them at the same time.

The Letting Year

As with most things, there is a rhythm to the ongoing processes associated with letting property. This is even more the case with letting property to students, where you have to fall in with the academic year that universities use. This chapter is an overview of what you need to do or consider throughout the year and refers you to the appropriate chapter in the book to take you through the fine detail.

January (or a month before the local university's property listing date)	Contact your existing tenants and ask them if they want to stay on. If they do, sign them up by the end of the month. If they don't, arrange viewing days with them.	Chapter 5
	Complete the annual registration form sent by your local university, or register with them if you are not already registered.	Chapter 5
	Check rent received from existing tenants.	Chapter 8
	Do second interim inspection and see to any defects.	Chapter 8

February	Your property is advertised. Give details to enquirers and arrange viewings.	Chapter 5
	Carry out reference checks and sign up your new group for the next academic year. Take deposits and check they clear. Get tenancy stamped if necessary.	Chapter 6
	Check rent received from existing tenants.	Chapter 8
March	Check rent received from existing tenants.	Chapter 8
April	If your existing tenants are moving out in June, prepare to serve them with a Section 21 Notice now.	Chapter 9
	Check rent received.	Chapter 8
	Do third interim inspection and deal with any defects.	Chapter 8
May	Send tenants the Moving Out checklist.	Chapter 9
	Check rent received.	Chapter 8
	Now is a good time to purchase property if you are considering letting to students for the next academic year.	Chapter 2

June–Aug	Notify utility companies and local council of tenants' moving out date and names of tenants moving in.	Chapter 9
	Double check with new tenants the date and time they will be checking in.	Chapter 7
	Carry out check-out with tenants, take meter readings and return deposits or notify them of deductions.	Chapter 9
	Check all rent received before releasing deposits.	
	Arrange for any work, cleaning, annual jobs, etc to be done before new tenants move in.	Chapter 7
	Update inventory and house pack.	Chapter 7
July–mid September	Meet new tenants for check-in, show round property, give them inventory and house pack and take meter readings.	Chapter 7
	Notify utility companies of meter readings.	Chapter 7
September	Do tax return.	Chapter 2
October	Do first interim inspection and deal with any defects.	Chapter 8
November	Now is the peak time for any interim voids that may crop up.	Chapter 8
December	Remind tenants of procedures to take if they are going home for a few weeks at Xmas.	Chapter 8

Useful Contacts

Association of Residential Letting Agents (ARLA)

Maple House

53–55 Woodside Road

Amersham

Bucks HP6 6AA

Tel: 0845 345 5752

www.arla.co.uk

ARLA is the professional and regulatory body for letting agents. Unfortunately, not many agents belong to it, but ARLA should be able to provide a list of those in your area who do.

CORGI (Council of Registered Gas Installers)

1 Elmwood

Chineham Business Park

Crockford Lane

Basingstoke

Hants RH24 8WG

Tel: 0870 401 2300

www.trustcorgi.com

Useful for finding qualified gas installers in your area.

The Court Service

www.hmcourts-service.gov.uk

An extremely useful site if you are unfortunate enough to have to consider taking legal action against your tenants. If you register, it is possible to start claims on line. Gives addresses of all regional county courts.

Department for Communities and Local Government

Tel: 0207 944 4400

www.communities.gov.uk

This is the government department responsible for most housing legislation, so it is a good one to bookmark. It also provides an easy link to each local authority website.

Electrical Contractors Association (ECA)

Tel: 0207 313 400

www.eca.co.uk

For information on registered electrical installers (see also NICEIC below)

FSA (The Financial Services Authority)

Tel: 0845 606 1234

www.moneymadeclear.fsa.gov.uk

The UK's financial watchdog and also provides lots of useful financial information.

Health and Safety Executive (HSE)

Tel: 0870 154 5500

www.hse.gov.uk

Produces information on health and safety, including gas and fire safety.

HM Revenue and Customs

www.hmrc.gov.uk

For general tax information and completing self-assessment on line.

Information on house prices and trends around the country
www.hometrack.co.uk
www.rightmove.co.uk

The Law Commission
www.lawcom.gov.uk
This is the department advising on reforms in tenancy law.

National Association of Citizens Advice Bureaux
Tel: 0207 833 2181
www.nacab.org.uk

National Inspection Council for Electrical Installation Contracting (NICEIC)
Tel: 0207 564 2323
www.niceic.org.uk

The Office of Fair Trading (OFT)
Tel: 0800 389 3158
www.oft.gov.uk
For copies of leaflets and reports on fair trading terms.

The Universities and Colleges Admissions Service
www.ucas.co.uk
Deals with applications for UK universities and has an easy to use database of all universities with key facts relating to student numbers, drop out rates and percentage of first year students housed by the institution.

LANDLORD ORGANISATIONS

It is always useful to have the support of an organisation committed to helping landlords. Contact the organisations below to find a branch that covers your area. Most will offer regular meetings, publications and advice, as well as standard tenancies and forms.

National Landlords Association
Tel: 0870 241 0471
www.landlords.org.uk

Residential Landlords Association
Tel: 0845 666 5000
www.rla.org.uk

National Federation of Residential Landlords
Tel: 0845 456 0357
www.nfrl.org.uk

Scottish Association of Landlords
Tel: 0131 270 4774
www.scottishlandlords.com

Landlords' Association of Northern Ireland
Tel: 0289 033 1644
www.lani.org.uk

Appendix 1

Inventory

INVENTORY

Property Address

Check-in date: ....

Meter readings:

    Electric:..

    Gas: ....

    Water: ....

Useful information

Electric meter location:	Hall cupboard
Gas meter location:	Outside front foor
Water meter location:	N/A
Boiler location:	In kitchen

Abbreviations for condition:

VG	= very good
G	= good
CWT	= certain wear and tear
P	= poor

Communal area

Curtains	with lining, G
Dining table	wooden, G
Chairs	4 wooden, G

Easy chairs	4, green covers, G
Carpets	beige, no stains, G
Lampshades	1G
Coffee table	1 wooden, G
Wall unit	dark wood, G
Radiator	G
Telephone point	
General decoration	cream walls, 2 marks on wall near fireplace, G overall

Hall/stairs/landing

Mirror	silver frame, G
Carpets	blue, G
Smoke detector	1
Lampshades	2 wall lamps, G and 1 VG lampshade
General decoration	white walls, G

Bedrooms	1	2	3	4
Bed (single)	1G	1G	1G	1G
Bed (double)				
Mattress	1G	1G	1G	1G
Wardrobe (f/s)	1CWT	1CWT		
Wardrobe (b/i)			1CWT	1CWT
Mirror				
Desk	1G	1G	1G	1G
Chair	1G	1G	1G	1G
Chest of drawers	1G	1G	1G	
Curtains	G	G	G	G
Lampshades	1G	1G	1 spot	1G
Carpets	G	G	G	G
Sink	1G			

General decoration	G	G	G	G

Bathroom/WC

Mirror	1G
Blinds	1G
Flooring	vinyl G
Shower curtain	new

Kitchen

Curtains/blinds	G
Cooker (electric)	Moffat
Hob	Neff 40
Hood	Turbo VG
Fridge/freezer	Zanussi 2F 67/44
Washing machine	Hoover Ecologic 800
Vacuum cleaner	1 Panasonic, serviced July 2006
Broom	1
Dustpan/brush	1
Bowl	1
Bin	1
Drainer	1
Mop/bucket	1
Lampshades	2 spots
Fire blanket	1 unused
Mat	G
Vinyl	tiled floor, G condition
General decoration	G

Outside

Dustbins	2
Washing line	1

Garden: lawn and flowerbeds, tidy and grass cut.

I confirm this inventory is correct at the check-in date stated on the front page.

Signed (landlord) .... **Date:** ....

Signed (for tenants)............................ **Date:** ....

Appendix 2

Tenant Application Form

APPLICATION FOR (*insert property address*)

APPLICANT DETAILS

Name ....

Email .... **Tel** ....

University ID number ....

Home address..

....

Previous landlord details for reference request

....

....

Name ....

Email .... **Tel** ....

University ID number ....

Home address..

....

Previous landlord details for reference request

....

....

Name ....

Email .... **Tel** ....

University ID number ....

Home address..

....

Previous landlord details for reference request

....

....

Name ....

Email .... **Tel**..........................

University ID number ....

Home address ....

....

Previous landlord details for reference request

....

....

Appendix 3

Reference Request Letter

A Landlord
39 Little Street, Anytown
AB1 2YZ

Tel: 03453-456789
Fax: 03453-457869

31 May 2006

AnyLet Agency Ltd
Fax: 03453-321567

Dear Sir/Madam

Reference request for Angela Jones and Simon Smith, 22 Tinpan Alley, Anytown AB1 3XY

The above named tenants have authorised me to approach you for a reference as to their suitability as future tenants of my property. I would be grateful if you could answer the following questions:

1. Are either of the above tenants currently in rent arrears? If so, please could you let me know how much they owe.

    ....

2. Have either of the above tenants been repeatedly late in paying their rent? (i.e. more than three times during the course of the tenancy)

....

3. To the best of your knowledge, has the property been kept in a tenant-like manner?

....

4. Have you received noise complaints from any neighbours of the above property relating to this tenancy?

....

5. Would you be happy to enter into another tenancy agreement with each of the above named tenants?

....

Signed: ....Landlord/Agent

Many thanks for your time in completing this form.

Yours faithfully

Andrew Landlord

Appendix 4

Property Inspection Report

Bedrooms	Double glazing	Central heating	Floors
1–5	Full/partial/none	Gas/elec/oil/coal/none	1–3
☐	☐	☐ Boiler location_____	☐

Condition: G = Good   CWT = Certain wear and tear   P = Poor   (V = very)

Room:	**Furniture** (condition)	**Decoration** (condition)	**Safety** (condition)
Living room	☐	☐	☐
Kitchen Washing machine? ☐	☐	☐	☐
Bedroom 1 Sink or ensuite? ☐	☐	☐	☐
Bedroom 2 Sink or ensuite? ☐	☐	☐	☐
Bedroom 3 Sink or ensuite? ☐	☐	☐	☐
Bedroom 4 Sink or ensuite? ☐	☐	☐	☐
Bedroom 5 Sink or ensuite? ☐	☐	☐	☐

Bathroom 1 Basin ☐ Bath ☐ WC ☐ Shower ☐ Dec ☐ Cond ☐

Bathroom 2 Basin ☐ Bath ☐ WC ☐ Shower ☐ Dec ☐ Cond ☐

Rear garden ☐ Grass/patio   **Front garden** ☐ Grass/patio

1. Outside of premises

Pipes – loose, coming away from wall? ☐

Tiles – loose, missing? ☐

Drains – blocked, leaking? ☐

Paint work – is the paint flaking? ☐

Windows – do they fit properly? Are there any gaps? ☐

Fences – are all the panels in place? ☐

Other

2. Halls and stairs

Lighting – is there adequate lighting? ☐

Carpeting and stair treads – in good condition? ☐

Banisters – firm and no missing supports? ☐

Sockets OK? ☐

Decorations?   good/fair/poor ☐

Ventilation – signs of damp or condensation? ☐

Smoke alarm? ☐

Other ☐

3. Kitchen

Sink – blocked? ☐

Taps – do they turn on/off? Leaky? ☐

Tiles – are there any missing/cracked? ☐

Flooring – does it cover all the floor? ☐

Is it coming away from the floor? ☐

Fire safety equipment – fire blanket/extinguishers ☐

Kitchen appliances – cooker gas/elec, wash mach etc, vacuum
    cleaner ☐

Windows – window catches? Do they open/close? ☐

Light – is there adequate lighting? Do all lights work? ☐

Ventilation – signs of damp or condensation? ☐

Electrical sockets? ☐

Fire door to kitchen with closer and seals OK? ☐

Other ☐

4. Living room

Ventilation – signs of damp or condensation? ☐

Windows – do they open/close? Locks? Do they fit properly? ☐

Curtains and curtain rails? ☐

Floor coverings – good condition? ☐

Light – is there adequate light? Do all lights work? ☐

No. of electric sockets? ☐

Radiators/valves? ☐

Furniture – good condition? ☐

Other ☐

5. Bathroom

Signs of leaking? ☐

Is the toilet leaky and does it flush? ☐

Bath – check edge seal/chips? ☐

Tiles – are there any missing or cracked? ☐

Taps – turn off/on and no leaks? ☐

Ventilation – signs of damp or condensation? ☐

Is the hot water coming through? ☐

Does shower work? ☐

Other ☐

6. Separate WC

Signs of flooding? ☐

Is the toilet leaky? Does it flush? ☐

Sink – check edge seals/chips? ☐

Tiles – are there any missing or cracked? ☐

Ventilation – signs of damp or condensation? ☐

Other ☐

7. Bedrooms

	1	2	3	4	5
Front/rear/side? (F/R/S)	☐	☐	☐	☐	☐
Décor	☐	☐	☐	☐	☐
Ventilation – signs of damp or condensation?	☐	☐	☐	☐	☐
Windows – do they open/close?	☐	☐	☐	☐	☐
Curtains and curtain rails?	☐	☐	☐	☐	☐
Floor coverings – are there carpets?	☐	☐	☐	☐	☐
Electrics – bare wires? damaged plugs?	☐	☐	☐	☐	☐
Radiator/valves adequate heating?	☐	☐	☐	☐	☐
Furniture – OK?	☐	☐	☐	☐	☐
Lighting – adequate? natural light?	☐	☐	☐	☐	☐
Sockets OK?	☐	☐	☐	☐	☐
Door closes OK?	☐	☐	☐	☐	☐

General notes

Appendix 5

Transfer of Tenancy Form

This transfer dated   is made between (1) the Landlord (2) the Continuing Tenant (3) the Outgoing Tenant and (4) the Incoming Tenant referred to in the following Particulars:

THE PARTICULARS

Landlord	Name	Home/present address
Continuing tenant(s)	1. 2. 3. 4.	
Outgoing tenant		
Incoming tenant		
The premises (as in the agreement)		
The agreement	Agreement dated for the letting of the Premises by the Landlord to [the Continuing Tenant and the Outgoing Tenant] (*)	

(*) insert name(s) of original Tenant(s) if not the same people as in square brackets.

1. In the transfer the singular shall include the plural where appropriate.

2. The Continuing Tenant and the Outgoing Tenant, with the consent of the Landlord, transfer the benefit of the Agreement to the Continuing Tenant and the Incoming Tenant.

3. The Landlord releases the Outgoing Tenant from all liability under the Agreement.

4. The Incoming Tenant agrees with the Landlord to observe jointly and severally with the Continuing Tenant the obligations on the part of the original Tenant contained in the Agreement.

5. The Outgoing Tenant acknowledges the receipt from the Incoming Tenant of £   being the Outgoing Tenant's share of the deposit held by the Landlord under the Agreement.

	Signed by:	Witness:
The Landlord	....	....
The Continuing Tenants	....	....
	....	....
	....	....
	....	....
The Outgoing Tenant	....	....
The Incoming Tenant	....	....

Appendix 6

Notice seeking possession of a property let on an assured shorthold tenancy (Section 21 Notice)

Assured Shorthold Tenancy: Notice Requiring Possession

To: (tenant's name)
Of: (property address)

From: (landlord's name)
Of: (landlord's address)

I give you notice that I require possession of the premises you are renting at: .... (address of property) on .... (date at expiry of correct notice period – at least 8 weeks/ 2 months).

Dated (date served) ....

Landlord's signature ....

(Landlord's name) ....

(Landlord's address) ....
....

Index